COMPLETE CLOSE READING
BOOK 3

JENNY THOMAS
DIANE WHITE

NELSON
CENGAGE Learning™

Australia • Brazil • Japan • Korea • Mexico • Singapore • Spain • United Kingdom • United States

Complete Close Reading Book 3
1st Edition
Jenny Thomas
Diane White

Cover designer: Book Design Ltd
Text designer: Book Design Ltd
Proofreader: Eva Chan
Production controller: Siew Han Ong

Any URLs contained in this publication were checked for currency during the production process. Note, however, that the publisher cannot vouch for the ongoing currency of URLs.

Acknowledgements
Our grateful thanks to all past and present colleagues who have so generously shared their expertise, creativity and resources. English departments thrive on your collegiality.
The authors and publisher wish to thank the following people and organisations for permission to use the resources in this textbook. Every effort has been made to trace and acknowledge all copyright owners of material used in this book. In most cases this was successful and copyright is acknowledged as requested. However, if any infringement has occurred the publishers tender their apologies and invite the copyright holders to contact them.

Page 8, *Geronimo Stilton #45 Save the White Whale* courtesy of Scholastic Inc and Atlantyca S.p.A; page 10, What's the greenest way to dry your hands? courtesy of *Green Ideas* magazine; page 14, Chocolate Beetroot Cake recipe courtesy of Food in a Minute and Heinz Wattie's Ltd; page 20, Mt Zion film (text and image) courtesy of the New Zealand Herald; page 22, Coronet Peak Trail Map courtesy of Coronet Peak Ski Area; page 24, WSPA advertisement courtesy of WSPA New Zealand; page 26, The Last Ocean by Rebekah White's courtesy of *Good* magazine, Issue 28, Jan/Feb 2003, Tangible Media. Images courtesy of Peter Young; page 28, Two Hands bread advertisement courtesy of George Weston Foods (NZ) Limited; page 32, Waihi Beach Shop Managers reckon they may make the country's biggest hamburger (text and image) courtesy of the New Zealand Herald; page 34, Brewers Dictionary of Phrase and Fable courtesy of Chambers Harrap publishers, UK; page 38, Hobbit's LA premiere still a winner for NZ courtesy of the New Zealand Herald; page 40, Fractures and dislocations (text and images) courtesy of St John New Zealand; page 42, *The Last Wolf speaks from the Zoo* courtesy of Pie Corbett; page 44, *Mud, Sweat and Tears* by Bear Grylls courtesy of William Morrow, UK; page 46, Lone Star advertisement courtesy of Lone Star; page 48, *The Keeper* courtesy of Barry Faville; page 50, BurgerFuel advertisement courtesy of BurgerFuel New Zealand; page 52, *Bargaining on Making a Difference*, *Toyota Believe* magazine, Issue 7, 2013 courtesy of Toyota New Zealand; page 54, Enrol and vote for the first time courtesy of Electoral Commission New Zealand; page 56, Karetu School mural project (text and image) courtesy of Karetu School; page 58, *Behind the Scenes* courtesy of Banjo Patterson; page 60, Powhiri text courtesy of Ross N Himona and Te Aute Publications Ltd; page 62, *Bird's Eye Guides Day Walks In NZ 100 Great Tracks* by Shaun Barnett (text and images) courtesy of Craig Potton Publishing; page 64, Magic Makeover courtesy of *New Zealand Girlfriend* magazine; page 66, *The Hunger Games* by Susanne Collins courtesy of Scholastic Inc; page 68, *Niu Sila* by David Armstrong and Oscar Kightley, courtesy of authors and Playmarket; page 70, *Tawera, Storyteller: Poems 1988-1999* by Simon Williamson courtesy of HeadworX Publishers, Wellington, 2002; page 72, *Grumpy Old Men - 47 Kiwi blokes, who've been around long enough to know, tell you what's wrong with the world* courtesy of Paul Little Books; page 74, *Heriot* by Margaret Mahy courtesy of Faber and Faber, UK; page 76, *Acquainted with the Night* by Robert Frost courtesy of Henry Holt, US; page 78, It may be English but it's not always as we know it by Stewart Riddle and The Conversation (theconversation.com).

For product information and technology assistance,
in Australia call **1300 790 853**;
in New Zealand call **0800 449 725**

For permission to use material from this text or product, please email **aust.permissions@cengage.com**

National Library of New Zealand Cataloguing-in-Publication Data
Thomas, Jenny, 1972-
Complete close reading. Book 3 / Jenny Thomas and Diane White.
ISBN 978-017026-012-1
1. Reading comprehension—Problems, exercises, etc.—Juvenile literature. [1. Reading comprehension—Problems, exercises, etc.]
I. White, Diane. II. Title.
428.43076—dc 23

Cengage Learning Australia
Level 7, 80 Dorcas Street
South Melbourne, Victoria Australia 3205

Cengage Learning New Zealand
Unit 4B Rosedale Office Park
331 Rosedale Road, Albany, North Shore 0632, NZ

For learning solutions, visit **cengage.com.au**

Printed in Australia by Ligare Pty Limited.
4 5 6 7 8 9 10 22 21 20 19 18

CONTENTS

ISBN 9780170260121

To the teacher …

As teachers of English we know that a student's ability to effectively and efficiently read, understand, analyse, interpret and respond to text is a significant focus in the senior English classroom. Therefore we appreciate the need to begin teaching students the basic skills required to effectively read and understand a text in our junior classes. *Complete Close Reading 3* provides a consistent approach to developing and practising the vitally important skills of reading with comprehension and/or responding to written, visual and oral texts.

Although the focus of many current assessments is strongly geared towards the achieved, merit, excellence system, *Complete Close Reading 3* holds to the idea that you can't run before you walk and, therefore, divides its questions into sections that bring together the best ideas from standards-based assessment, three level reading guides and the tried and tested straightforward comprehension questions approach to give you a textbook that focuses on developing those essential skills rather than the final summative assessment. It would be expected that you as a teacher (and school examinations) would reflect an individual school's assessment and reporting methods.

Each unit is organised into five sections:

On the surface

These are basic literal questions. Students should be able to find the answer clearly written in the text.

Discovering techniques

These are questions about the purpose, structure and features of the text. Students will need to focus on the intended audience, the language used and the way the text has been constructed.

Search and think

These are inferential or interpretive questions. Students will have to use their own knowledge and thinking, as well as information from the text, to answer questions in this section.

Hidden depths

These are creative, critical or higher-order-thinking questions. Students will need to respond to this section as individuals and be prepared to justify their responses.

Extend yourself

These are more open-ended questions. They provide a range of opportunities for students to respond to the text at a deeper level by writing, viewing, listening and speaking. As the title of the section suggests, these would be most useful as extension, homework, extended absences or last period on a Friday afternoon.

Complete Close Reading 3 provides good models of a wide range of text types, incorporating many areas of secondary school study.

Complete Close Reading 3 acknowledges the importance of difference and diversity in both the texts selected and in the opportunity for teachers and students to tailor the use of each unit to cater for individual differences in ability, language background and learning style. Teachers are encouraged to assist students to decide which questions are most appropriate for their ability, preferred learning styles and the time available. *Complete Close Reading 3* can be used in class for individual, group or whole class work and at home for homework and revision.

Students may respond well to being given marks for a change and some teachers like to give marks as formative assessment, so optional assessment has been given in the first three sections of each unit. It is based on a simple one mark per question (or dictionary definition) formula. Please use your judgement when it comes to awarding half marks. You may even like to put a 'bonus' mark against some questions that would be challenging for your students.

We hope you enjoy using the variety of texts explored in *Complete Close Reading 3* and assisting students to take literacy into many areas of school and life.

ISBN 9780170260121

How to ... close read

Complete Close Reading 3 presents you with a variety of texts and asks you questions about those texts to ensure that you understand what you are reading. Your ability to effectively and efficiently read, understand and interpret written text is a significant focus in the senior English classroom; therefore you need to begin learning the basic skills required to do this effectively in your junior classes.

The questions are divided into categories to lead you through a text, from straightforward factual questions to ones that want you to think a little more. Here are the categories:

1 On the surface

One of the skills close reading tests is your ability to understand what is happening in the text. Therefore the first type of question you will meet is the basic literal question where the answer is clearly written in the text.

They are likely to be based around 'facts'. Things such as:

- Who
- What
- When
- Where
- Why
- How.

In other words, you will be looking for factual information.

2 Discovering techniques

You are going to hear the word 'style' quite often when you study English. It means the way something has been written. To help you understand the writer's craft, you will begin by looking at the techniques the writer has used to create their text. This will include things like vocabulary – the words selected by the writer, and structure – the way the sentences are ordered. You will also be asked to identify the basic language features.

To answer these successfully you will need to have some idea about the intended audience, be able to recognise the language used and the way the text has been put together.

To help you out we have included a list of Language Terms on page 80.

3 Search and think

You will have to 'read between the lines' of the text to answer questions in this section. It is likely you will need to use your own knowledge and thinking, as well as information from the text, to answer these questions.

For many of you these will be the trickiest of the questions because they demand that you think carefully about what is being said and then think about what that means. You may think this is difficult but in fact you do it every day. You look at people's body language, tone of voice, the words they choose to use and then you make a judgement on how you will respond. These questions ask you to do the same thing. Read the passage and make a judgement of what is being implied rather than openly stated. Hence you will have to 'read between the lines' of the text to answer questions.

4 Hidden depths

These questions want you to go beyond the text and respond in a personal way to it. You may be asked to be creative or to look for links to your own experiences or opinions.

5 Extend yourself

These questions are for when there is time and opportunity to undertake research on ideas or projects that develop from the text. They may encourage further, wider reading or offer you pathways that lead on from the text's starting point.

How to … close read a written text

We know you have probably been told this many times already but we thought that we would remind you one more time!

Before you begin

Look carefully at the surrounding information. Focus on the text type and:

- think about where and why these text types are used.
- recall any prior experience with this type of text or this topic.
- predict what the text may be about and how it is likely to be structured.

Read once

Read the text carefully. Try to visualise what is happening in the text.

Scan

Scan the text for difficult or unfamiliar words or phrases. Work out the meanings for this vocabulary by using the context of the passage or consulting a dictionary.

Read again

- Notice any language features the author has used.
- Note other effective words and phrases.
- Note any special sentence structures.
- What do these things add to your understanding?
- Think about the tone created in the passage.
- Is there a particular style?

Remember, this is not a race!

Answer the questions

Work through the questions one at a time. Remember two important skills:

1. Scanning: Where instead of reading word for word, your eyes are searching quickly through something looking for a specific thing. Some people use their finger or a ruler to help them scan.
2. Skimming: Most commonly used to 'skim read' a written text to locate relevant information.
   a. Start by identifying the key words (scanning) in the questions, which will show you where the answers are in the text.
   b. Then skim read the text by sliding your eyes down the middle of the page or moving your finger across the page looking for key words.
   c. When you find the key word, quickly read around it to find the answer to the question.

When you write your answers, try to be as clear and as detailed as possible. It is always good to explain the reason for your answer.

  ISBN 9780170260121

How to … close read a visual text

Although there are many features that are similar between any text you close read, visual text have some unique features that we thought we would remind you about.

When close reading a visual text you need to keep in mind:

- Who/What is being advertised/presented (product/service/message).
- Who is being targeted (audience).
- What is the overall idea we are intended to get from the text (message).

Next is to remember that a majority of visual text you will study can be broken down into elements:

- Headline — tone, message, font choice, size
- Image — subject, layout, colours
- Body copy — vocabulary choice, tone, mood, language techniques, emotive language
- Background — colour, empty space, pattern
- Logo — philosophy, symbol, colours
- Slogan — language techniques

You will need to look carefully at each of these parts when you analyse an image.

What are you looking for?

As with the other text you are learning to analyse, there are techniques that are commonly found within visual text. These can be divided into two categories – those that deal with the written aspects of the text (verbal) and those that deal with the visual element (visual). You will often be asked to find links between verbal and visual techniques.

VISUAL	***VERBAL***
Font (style and size)	*Headline*
Colour	*Type of language (formal, informal, colloquial, slang, jargon)*
Dominant Visual Feature (DVF)	*Body copy*
Layout	*Repetition*
Bold lines	*Use of adjectives*
Empty space	*Personal pronouns*
Contrast	*Rhetorical question*
Unusual images	*Alliteration*
Background	*Slogan*
Symbols/logos	

ISBN 9780170260121

UNIT 1

TEXT TYPE Junior Fiction/Narrative (extract)
PURPOSE To tell a story
STRUCTURE
1 Orientation
2 Complication
3 Series of events
4 Resolution

FEATURES Simple vocabulary and sentence structure, descriptive language, characters, illustration

HE'S A MESS!

Lulled by the sound of the WAVES, I was about to drift off to sleep. But suddenly, three FRAIL voices woke me up.

"It's him, Gladys."

"Are you sure, Mitzi?"

"You ask him, Gertrude."

"Excuse me, aren't you Geronimo Stilton, the bigshot newspaper mouse?"

I opened my eyes.

Three old ladies stood over me.

"Um, yes, I'm Geronimo Stilton," I said.

"He's much better looking in photos, don't you agree, Mitzi?" the first mouse commented.

"Oh, definitely, Gertrude," the second mouse said. "Look at his fur. It's all *knotted*.

And what's with his eyes? Are they crossed? What do you think, Gladys?"

"He's a  mess," the third mouse announced.

I sighed. I felt a pounding headache coming on.

"Sorry to disappoint you," I said.

I was about to close my eyes again when one of the old ladies pulled out a HUGE stack of papers.

"Even though you're a mesS, we still want your autograph. Can you sign one for each of us, and one for all our friends?" she asked.

I gulped.

If my eyes weren't crossed now, they would be by the time I finished signing all of those sheets. It would take me **hours**!

But what could I do? After all, I am a gentlemouse.

With a sigh, I bent my head and started signing.

Oh, what a miserable vacation!

On the surface *(Literal comprehension – right-there questions)*

1 Who was drifting off to sleep on the beach?
2 Which old lady thinks the newspaper mouse is not good looking in real life?
3 What do the old ladies criticise about his appearance?
4 What sort of pen does he use to sign the autographs?
5 Why does he think his holiday is imperfect?

Discovering techniques *(Language structures and features, spelling, grammar, vocabulary)*

1 Use a dictionary to find the meaning of the following words as they are used in the text:
   a lulled
   b frail
   c bigshot.
2 This book is written for an audience of 8-11 year olds. Comment on the way font shape and colour have been used with this audience in mind.
3 What other ways have the authors and designers of this book tried to appeal to their audience?

Search and think *(Inferential and interpretive comprehension)*

1 The writer uses several verbs to describe speech. List them. Why does he do this?
2 The old ladies have many friends. How do we know this?
3 Why has the author chosen the name Geronimo Stilton for his lead character?

Hidden depths *(Creative comprehension – responding personally, higher-order-thinking skills, making links)*

1 Read the chapter aloud to another person in your class or to a younger person. Do the voices!
2 Create a character based on an animal for a similar story of your own. Write the first chapter of a story using this character.
3 Find a Geronimo Stilton story and read it all. Even though you are not the target audience, are there features of the story that you still find appealing?
4 Research what a children's author has to think about when writing a book for younger children.

Extend yourself *(Links to real life or other literature, researching, writing, creating, speaking tasks)*

1 Research how many stories for children (or adults) use animals as characters. Start with what you and your classmates can think of *before* turning to the Internet.
2 Create a Geronimo Stilton story (or one based on your character) and create a story book for a younger child. Include lots of pictures and unusual fonts like this extract uses.

ISBN 9780170260121

UNIT 2

TEXT TYPE Discussion

PURPOSE To inform and persuade by presenting evidence and opinions about more than one side of an issue

STRUCTURE Opening statement presenting the issue
Arguments or evidence for different points of view
Concluding recommendation

FEATURES Facts and figures, logical reasoning, examples, persuasive or emotive language

what's the greenest way to dry your hands?

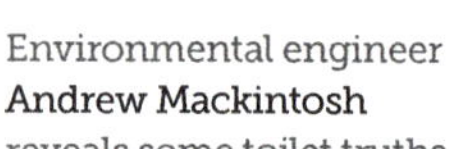

Environmental engineer **Andrew Mackintosh** reveals some toilet truths

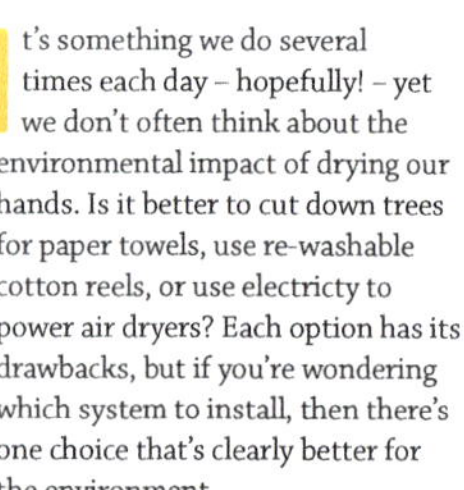

It's something we do several times each day – hopefully! – yet we don't often think about the environmental impact of drying our hands. Is it better to cut down trees for paper towels, use re-washable cotton reels, or use electricty to power air dryers? Each option has its drawbacks, but if you're wondering which system to install, then there's one choice that's clearly better for the environment.

Sources: Öko-institut e.V. 13 June 2006. A comparison of cotton towels and paper towels. Environmental Resources Management. August 2001. Study Prepared for Airdri Ltd. and Bobrick Washroom Equipment Inc.. Streamlined Life Cycle Assessment. Öko-Institut e.V. 13 June 2006. Total Environmental Burden – Life Cycle Analysis on hand-drying system. Massachusetts Institute of Technology. 19 September 2011. Life Cycle Assessment of Hand Drying Systems. Climate Change Office, NZ. August 2003. Electricity Emission Factor. Keith Redway & Shameem Fawdar. February 2009. A comparative study of different hand drying methods: paper towel, warm air drier, Dyson Airblade® drier. School of Biosciences University of Westminster London. INTERMETRA Business & Market Research Group. June 2008. Study of the Consumers' Attitudes to Different Handdrying Systems for European Tissue Symposium.

THE VERDICT – what's greener?

Cold-air 'blade' dryers are by far the greenest option – followed by hot air dryers and cotton reels. Disposable paper towels have the worse environmental impact of all the methods. If you have to use paper towels insist on a brand that carries FSC, PEFC or ECNZ certification, which ensures the trees they're made from were grown sustainably.

PAPER TOWELS	COTTON REELS	HOT-AIR DRYERS	COLD-AIR 'BLADE' DRYER
Made from wood pulp these can include anywhere between 0 and 100 per cent recycled content.	A reel of cotton inside a cabinet gives you a fixed length of clean towel to dry your hands on with each pull.	These dry your hands by evapourating the water with heated air.	This recent technology uses high-speed air 'blades' to scrape the wat from your hands, meaning the air doesn't need to be heated.
✗ The biggest impact of this system comes from making the paper (growing trees, plus the heavily industrial pulp and paper process), while disposal, transport and bin liners also contribute.	✗ Growing cotton conventionally uses large volumes of agrichemicals.	✓ Raw materials, manufacture, transport and disposal only account for about 5 per cent of the environmental impacts of these machines. The main impact comes from the electricty that powers them, which in New Zealand is a mostly renewable resource with low CO_2 emissions.	
✗ Paper towels can't normally be recycled as they're considered to be contaminated after use. However it is possible to compost them.	✓ Cotton reels can be reused 70-130 times before they wear out. ✗ However, each time they're re-used cotton reels are washed, which requires significant amounts of water, energy and cleaning chemicals. ✓ Once they've worn out, cotton reels are often cut up and used again as rags.		
✗ The equivalent of 18g of CO_2 is emitted for each time you dry your hands (using two towels).	The equivalent of 9.3g of CO_2 is emitted for each time you dry your hands (one pull).	The equivalent of 12g of CO_2 is emitted for each time you dry your hands (30 seconds).	✓ The equivalent of 3g of CO_2 is emitted for each time you dry your hands (12 seconds).

ISBN 9780170260121

On the surface *(Literal comprehension – right-there questions)*

1 How many options were tested?
2 What is a paper towel made from?
3 How many times can a cotton reel be reused?
4 How do hot-air dryers dry your hands?
5 Which option was considered 'greener'?

Optional Assessment: 5 x 1 mark = 5 marks

Discovering techniques *(Language structures and features, spelling, grammar, vocabulary)*

1 Find one example of each of the following techniques:
   a alliteration
   b comparative adjective
   c superlative adjective.
2 In the table, three different fill colours are used. Why?
3 What information is given in the fine print on the bottom left?

Optional Assessment: 5 x 1 mark = 5 marks

Search and think *(Inferential and interpretive comprehension)*

1 The article uses five photographs, not illustrations. Why?
2 What other visual features does the article use?
3 Do used paper towels have any good points?
4 What makes the Cold-air 'blade' dryer better for the environment than the Hot-air Dryer?

Optional Assessment: 4 x 1 mark = 4 marks

Hidden depths *(Creative comprehension – responding personally, higher-order-thinking skills, making links)*

1 Explain why if using paper towels we should pick those with FSC, PEFC and ECNZ certification. (You need to find out what these abbreviations mean first.)
2 Which option would you prefer to use and which option would you least prefer to use. Why?
3 Who would be most likely to use the information in this article? Explain your answer.
4 One thing that this research doesn't tell you is the price of each of these options. Do you think that people should/will consider only the environment in a situation like this? See if you can find out the prices of each option first.

Extend yourself *(Links to real life or other literature, researching, writing, creating, speaking tasks)*

1 Andrew Mackintosh is an 'Environmental Engineer'. Research what this job would involve.
2 Survey at least 30 people from different age groups on their preference of hand drying methods. (Use the four methods from the article.) Present the results on a graph.
3 Turn the information presented in this article into a 250 word formal essay or a speech.
4 Create an infographic for another choice people make that has environmental implications. For example, using paper or plastic or jute carrier bags at the supermarket; choosing a form of transport to go to school or work; or anything environmental you are concerned about.

ISBN 9780170260121

UNIT 3

TEXT TYPE Letter

PURPOSE To communicate information, experiences or ideas, formally or informally, in writing to a reader who is not present

STRUCTURE
1. Address and date
2. Greeting or salutation
3. Series of events or issues in paragraphs
4. Sign off

FEATURES Set layout, informal or formal language depending on purpose and audience, varied sentences

8B Splendid Court
Beauville
Taranaki

28 September 2013

The Principal
Beauville Primary School
Beauville
Taranaki

Dear Ms Sterling

I wish to congratulate your school for the way in which your students travel to and from their classrooms every day.

You can see by my address that I live in a property adjacent to the school and I watch the students coming and going each day. I have been pleasantly surprised to note that in almost every case those on bicycles wear their helmets, and wear them correctly.

I know from perusing the *Beauville Times Advertiser* that the number of ACC claims resulting from accidents on bikes is rising each year. You must be pleased that none of your pupils is involved in these numbers.

However, I am concerned that the same concern for personal safety does not extend to skateboarders. Very few of them wear helmets, although I am sure that there must be as many injuries from skateboard accidents as from bicycles.

When I was a girl my younger brother and I rode our bikes to and from school every day. Unfortunately one day he was in a rather nasty accident, he fell on the road and sustained serious head injuries. He has been affected by this injury for over 50 years, so I know what I am talking about.

If you would like a person to attend a school assembly to speak about these matters I am sure someone from the Safekids organisation would be pleased to assist.

Yours sincerely

Mrs Jean Sharpeye

  ISBN 9780170260121

On the surface *(Literal comprehension – right-there questions)*

1 What is the letter writer's name?
2 Where does she live?
3 What job does Ms Sterling do?
4 Who is Mrs Sharpeye worried about?
5 What happened when Mrs Sharpeye was a child that made her write this letter?

Discovering techniques *(Language structures and features, spelling, grammar, vocabulary)*

1 Explain why the word 'I' is used so often in this letter.
2 Find a compound word in this letter.
3 Use a dictionary to find the meanings of the following words as they are used in the text:
   a adjacent
   b perusing.
4 The writer uses an adverb to describe how the students wear their helmets. What is it?

Search and think *(Inferential and interpretive comprehension)*

1 What is the *Beauville Times Advertiser*?
2 What does the letter suggest about Mrs Sharpeye's own life?

Hidden depths *(Creative comprehension – responding personally, higher-order-thinking skills, making links)*

1 If you were the principal, how would you respond to Mrs Sharpeye's letter? Write your response.
2 How can we encourage skateboarders to wear helmets, too? Prepare a poster to try to do this.

Extend yourself *(Links to real life or other literature, researching, writing, creating, speaking tasks)*

1 Research the number of bike and skateboard riders at your school. Conduct an opinion poll about wearing helmets.
2 Find out what the accident statistics are in your area and present them as a diagram.
3 Is there an opposite case to be made? Lots of countries do not make bike riders wear helmets. Which ones? Select one country and find out why they do not have this rule.

UNIT 4

TEXT TYPE Procedure/Instructions

PURPOSE To give instructions or show how something is accomplished through a series of steps

STRUCTURE
1 Opening statement of goal or aim
2 Material required listed in order of use
3 Series of steps listed in chronological order

FEATURES Logical sequence of steps, may use technical language

Chocolate Beetroot Cake

serves: Makes 20 cm round cake ✱ 15 minutes prep time ✱ Approx. 60 minutes cook time

Ingredients

- 410 g can Wattie's Beetroot, sliced with no added salt
- 2 eggs
- ¾ cup oil (canola or any mild vegetable oil)
- 1 cup castor sugar
- 1 tsp vanilla extract
- 1¼ cups self-raising flour
- ½ tsp baking soda
- ¼ cup cocoa

METHOD

1. Preheat the oven to 170°C. Grease a 20 cm diameter cake tin and line the base with baking paper.
2. Drain the Wattie's Beetroot. Purée in a food processor or blender until smooth.
3. Put eggs, oil, castor sugar and vanilla extract into a mixing bowl. Beat together well. Mix in the beetroot purée. Sift the self-raising flour, baking soda and cocoa into the mixture and mix to combine. Pour into the prepared cake tin.
4. Bake for approximately 60 minutes or until a skewer inserted comes out clean and the cake has shrunk from the sides of the tin. Remove from the oven and allow to stand for 5 minutes before turning onto a cake rack to cool.
5. When the cake is cold, dust with icing sugar before serving or top with Chocolate Ganache.

Chocolate Ganache

Ingredients:
125 g dark chocolate
¼ cup cream

To make Chocolate Ganache:
Gently melt chocolate and cream in a small bowl over hot water until chocolate melts. Stir to combine. Allow to cool and thicken before pouring over the top of the cake.

  ISBN 9780170260121

On the surface *(Literal comprehension – right-there questions)*

1 How much preparation time is required?
2 What temperature do you need to preheat the oven to?
3 What do you use baking paper for?
4 What do you need to ensure about the beetroot you use?
5 How many ingredients are required to make Chocolate Ganache?

Discovering techniques *(Language structures and features, spelling, grammar, vocabulary)*

1 What do the following abbreviations stand for?
   a g
   b tsp
   c °C
2 What does the word 'ganache' mean?
3 What is a 'purée'? Which language does the word come from? When was it first used?
4 The recipe lists five steps to make the cake. Why is the adding of Chocolate Ganache not number six?

Search and think *(Inferential and interpretive comprehension)*

1 What do you have to have 'prepared' before you begin making this cake?
2 What appliances would you need to cook this recipe?
3 Why do Food in a Minute/Wattie's provide recipes?

Hidden depths *(Creative comprehension – responding personally, higher-order-thinking skills, making links)*

1 Is it possible to write a recipe without using words? Try to present this recipe as a cartoon or a poster.
2 Do people respond to advertising like this? Change the brand name to an unknown name (make it up) and ask people who bake – which recipe would you use? The one with the Wattie's beetroot or the one with the XXX beetroot?

Extend yourself *(Links to real life or other literature, researching, writing, creating, speaking tasks)*

1 Research why people use beetroot in a chocolate cake.
2 Many people enjoy strange combinations of foods. Ask around your friends, family and schoolmates. Make a chart to show the odd combinations people enjoy. If you can't find enough in your own world, use the Internet, but start with people you know first. (Ask your Mum what she liked to eat when she was pregnant with you!)
3 Find your family's best chocolate cake recipe. Make it and bring into class. Yum!

ISBN 9780170260121

TEXT TYPE Procedure/Instructions
PURPOSE To give instructions or show how something is accomplished through a series of steps
STRUCTURE
1 Opening statement of goal or aim
2 Material required listed in order of use
3 Series of steps listed in chronological order
FEATURES Logical sequence of steps, may use technical language and diagrams

M2: Metal Reactions

Prac 64: Conditions that cause rusting

Aim:

To find out what conditions cause rusting.

Gear:

Test tubes with bungs, 10 thick iron nails, anhydrous calcium chloride, olive oil.

What to do:

1 Set up test tubes in a rack as shown in the diagram.

Test tube 1 has nails in moist air and is called the control experiment because you will compare all the other results with it.

Test tube 2 has nails submerged in water that you have boiled to remove any dissolved air. The olive oil layer stops any air getting into the water.

Test tube 3 has nails sitting in water.

Test tube 4 has nails in a test tube with anhydrous calcium chloride, which removes moisture form the air.

Test tube 5 has nails sealed in a test tube with water and pure oxygen. You will have done a practical to make oxygen last year.

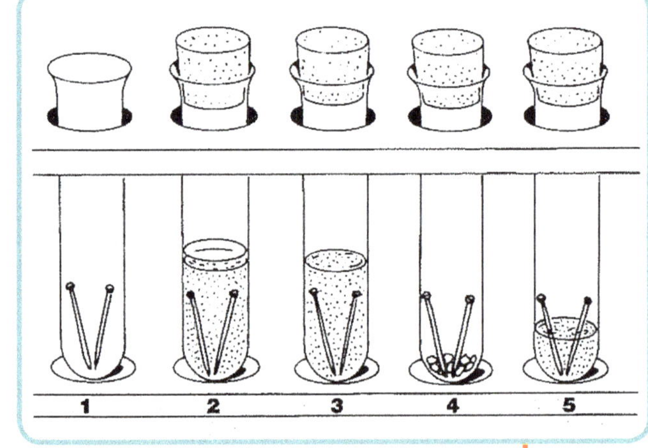

2 Leave the test tubes for several days, and enter your observations in the results table.

Results:

1 Complete the table below:

	Conditions	Amount of rust after 5 days
Tube 1		
Tube 2		
Tube 3		
Tube 4		
Tube 5		

2 Write down the two conditions that must exist for the iron to rust.

____

____

ISBN 9780170260121

On the surface *(Literal comprehension – right-there questions)*

1 What type of oil do you need to carry out this experiment?
2 How many test tubes do you need to carry out this experiment?
3 What does 'anhydrous calcium chloride' do?
4 What experiment will the students have done prior to this?
5 How long does this experiment run for?

Discovering techniques *(Language structures and features, spelling, grammar, vocabulary)*

1 Imperative verbs command you to do/perform an action, for example, 'Close that door'. Instructions rely on such verbs to make the procedure clear. Copy out three imperative verbs from the text.

Search and think *(Inferential and interpretive comprehension)*

1 There are other things that you need to complete this experiment that are not listed under the 'Gear' sub-heading. What are they?
2 Do you think that the diagram makes this experiment clearer? Explain your answer.
3 Read what is written vertically on the worksheet. Why are the words there?

Hidden depths *(Creative comprehension – responding personally, higher-order-thinking skills, making links)*

1 This is a very straightforward set of instructions. What would a student need to know in advance?
2 There are several reasons given in the instructions. What are they? Why are they included?
3 What do the words 'You will have done ...' suggest the writer assumes about his reader?
4 Do you like being given worksheets like this for experiments in class? Why/why not? Be honest!

Extend yourself *(Links to real life or other literature, researching, writing, creating, speaking tasks)*

1 Research the Internet for the conditions that cause rust on the Internet and choose the test tube that is most likely to be the one that produces the most rust.
2 Why do we need to know what causes rust? You might want to ask your parents!
3 Create a worksheet for an experiment a person could do at home. Aim to be as precise as this example.

ISBN 9780170260121

UNIT 6

TEXT TYPE Explanation

PURPOSE To inform, to explain how or why things are as they are, or how things work

STRUCTURE
1. A general statement
2. Series of statement or events in chronological or logical order
3. Concluding statement

FEATURES Logical sequence of details or ideas may use heading, diagrams and tables

What is the United Nations?

The United Nations officially came into existence on 24 October, 1945. The aims of the United Nations are to:

- keep peace throughout the world.
- develop friendly relations between nations.
- work together to help people live better lives, to eliminate poverty, disease and illiteracy in the world, to stop environmental destruction and to encourage respect for each other's rights and freedoms.
- be a centre for helping nations achieve the above aims.

There are currently 192 Members of the United Nations. They meet in the General Assembly, which is the closest thing to a world parliament. Each country, large or small, rich or poor, has a single vote, however, none of the decisions taken by the Assembly are binding. Nevertheless, the Assembly's decisions become resolutions that carry the weight of world governmental opinion.

The principles of the United Nations are:

- All Member States have sovereign equality.
- All Member States must obey the Charter.
- Countries must try to settle their differences by peaceful means.
- Countries must avoid using force or threatening to use force.
- The UN may not interfere in the domestic affairs of any country.
- Countries should try to assist the United Nations.

The United Nations Charter

The United Nations Charter gives the United Nations Security Council the power and responsibility to maintain international peace and security. This means they are in charge of peacekeeping operations. Peacekeepers monitor and observe peace processes in areas that have had conflict and assist ex-combatants in implementing the peace agreements they may have signed. New Zealand has a long history of being involved in UN peacekeeping operations.

United Nations peacekeepers (often referred to as Blue Berets because of their light blue berets or helmets) can include soldiers, police officers, and civilian personnel.

Most of these operations are established and implemented by the United Nations itself, with troops serving under UN operational control. In these cases, peacekeepers remain members of their respective armed forces, and do not constitute an independent 'UN army', as the UN does not have such a force.

ISBN 9780170260121

On the surface *(Literal comprehension – right-there questions)*

1 What year was the UN founded?
2 How many countries are members of the United Nations?
3 Where does the United Nations meet?
4 What is the role of the peacekeepers?
5 Why are they called the 'Blue Berets'?

Optional Assessment: 5 x 1 mark = 5 marks

Discovering techniques *(Language structures and features, spelling, grammar, vocabulary)*

1 'Peacekeepers', 'peacebuilding' and 'peacemaking' are all examples of what type of word?
2 A simple sentence has one clause, for example: The day is hot. A compound sentence has two main clauses linked by a conjunction, for example: The day is hot and the sky is blue. Go through the passage and copy out a compound sentence.

Optional Assessment: 2 x 1 mark = 2 marks

Search and think *(Inferential and interpretive comprehension)*

1 Why do you think the United Nations was begun in 1945?
2 How many votes does each country get? Why is this important?
3 What is meant by the phrase 'none of the decisions taken by the Assembly are binding'?
4 Why are United Nations decisions important?
5 Who do the Blue Berets work for?

Optional Assessment: 5 x 1 mark = 5 marks

Hidden depths *(Creative comprehension – responding personally, higher-order-thinking skills, making links)*

1 This is a clear, brief summary of the United Nations. Where do you think this passage would have been used?
2 Find out where New Zealand Blue Berets are working today. How many are from New Zealand's armed forces? Present your findings on a world map.
3 Why do you think it is important to have an organisation like the United Nations? Explain your answer.

Extend yourself *(Links to real life or other literature, researching, writing, creating, speaking tasks)*

1 The United Nations states it aims include promoting and facilitating co-operation of the following:
   - Promoting and facilitating co-operation in international law
   - International security
   - Economic development
   - Social progress
   - Human rights
   - Civil rights
   - Civil liberties
   - Political freedoms
   - Democracy
   - The achievement of lasting world peace.

   Research one of these and present your information graphically.
2 Research New Zealand's involvement in the United Nations.
3 Research the predecessor to the United Nations, the League of Nations. What happened to cause there to be a change?

ISBN 9780170260121

UNIT 7

TEXT TYPE Film review

PURPOSE To give details and opinion of a current film

STRUCTURE
1. Context – background information
2. Synopsis of plot, but not revealing ending
3. Opinion of reviewer
4. Recommendation, rating, director, actors

FEATURES Language may be formal or informal, depending on audience and type of film. May include description of setting, scenes, acting etc.

Appropriately for a movie which spends a fair bit of time in the potato fields of Pukekohe, *Mt Zion* is a bit of a mash-up. It's a family saga, a get-ahead-in-showbiz story, a late '70s time capsule and a musical tribute too - just as *Boy* had a thing for Michael Jackson, *Mt Zion* is for the love of Bob Marley.

And while cramming in all those ingredients can make for a lumpy mix of subplots, first-time feature director Tearepa Kahi serves it all up with obvious love, a quietly watchful pace and a sunbaked visual style.

The result is a smart, finely-observed, heartfelt drama of good humour and decent tunes against an authentic local setting. Sure, it does come with some artificial flavouring, care of the singing voice of Stan Walker, who plays young Marley-obsessed potato picker Turei. He sounds way too experienced too early in the film. And no, *Idol* star Walker hasn't missed his calling as an actor. But he's more than passable and ably supported, especially by his band-mates as well as Temuera Morrison as his father who puts in his best performance for quite some time.

It's set in 1979 when Marley and the Wailers came to Western Springs. Turei wants his band to enter the competition for the support slot.

But the paddocks on the southside of the Bombays aren't easily escaped, especially when your dad is the dutiful potato-picking gang boss ordering double shifts and your mum would rather you use your vocal talents welcoming dignitaries down at the local marae.

There are other hitches, like a lack of decent gear, an errant cousin shacked up in the city with one of the show's promoters, a family accident and dodgy local guitar hero 'Booker D' to deal with. Booker is played by Kevin Coco (formerly Kaukau), who gets to do a string-biting solo just like he did back in his Golden Harvest days, and his disco-era band also figures in this.

The original songs that Turei's band Small Axe perform are more soul-shaped than reggae-fired but they're still a solidly tuneful bunch, especially the title track. But one of the best tricks *Mt Zion* pulls off is evoking the Bob-spirit and his galvanising effect on Turei's generation without the need - or more probably the budget - to have his music on the soundtrack. Marley sure makes his presence felt and helps make this rough diamond of a film shine through its flaws. One that is sure to strike a chord with many. Especially those who know the ones to *Redemption Song* or *One Love*.

Stars:	4/5
Cast:	Stan Walker, Temuera Morrison, Miriama Smith
Rating:	PG (coarse language)
Director:	Tearepa Kahi
Running time:	93 mins
Verdict:	A film for the whole whanau

ISBN 9780170260121

On the surface *(Literal comprehension – right-there questions)*

1 Where is the film set?
2 When is the film set?
3 What is the name of the main character and the actor who plays that part?
4 What does the main character's mother want him to use his singing talent for?
5 Who directed the film?

Discovering techniques *(Language structures and features, spelling, grammar, vocabulary)*

1 The first paragraph includes a pun. Find it and explain its meaning.
2 What language technique continues this idea in the second paragraph?
3 Why is the word 'Idol' in italics?
4 Find two metaphors in the final paragraph.

Search and think *(Inferential and interpretive comprehension)*

1 This review has both good and bad things to say about the film. Find those opinion words and decide if the review is more positive than negative.
2 Consider the choice of vocabulary. Are any colloquial words used? In connection with which part of the review?
3 What does the reviewer consider to be the best part of the film?

Hidden depths *(Creative comprehension – responding personally, higher-order-thinking skills, making links)*

1 If this review was in a newspaper in Australia, which words might need explaining? Why?
2 What does a film reviewer have to be careful not to do in a review?
3 Would you go and see this film? How has the review affected your decision?

Extend yourself *(Links to real life or other literature, researching, writing, creating, speaking tasks)*

1 Create an advertisement for this film.
2 Watch the film. Write your own review.
3 Research the career of Temuera Morrison or Tearepa Kahi.

UNIT 8

TEXT TYPE Map
PURPOSE To show locations and features
STRUCTURE Pictorial representation of a region
FEATURES Visual information, combining words, symbols and images

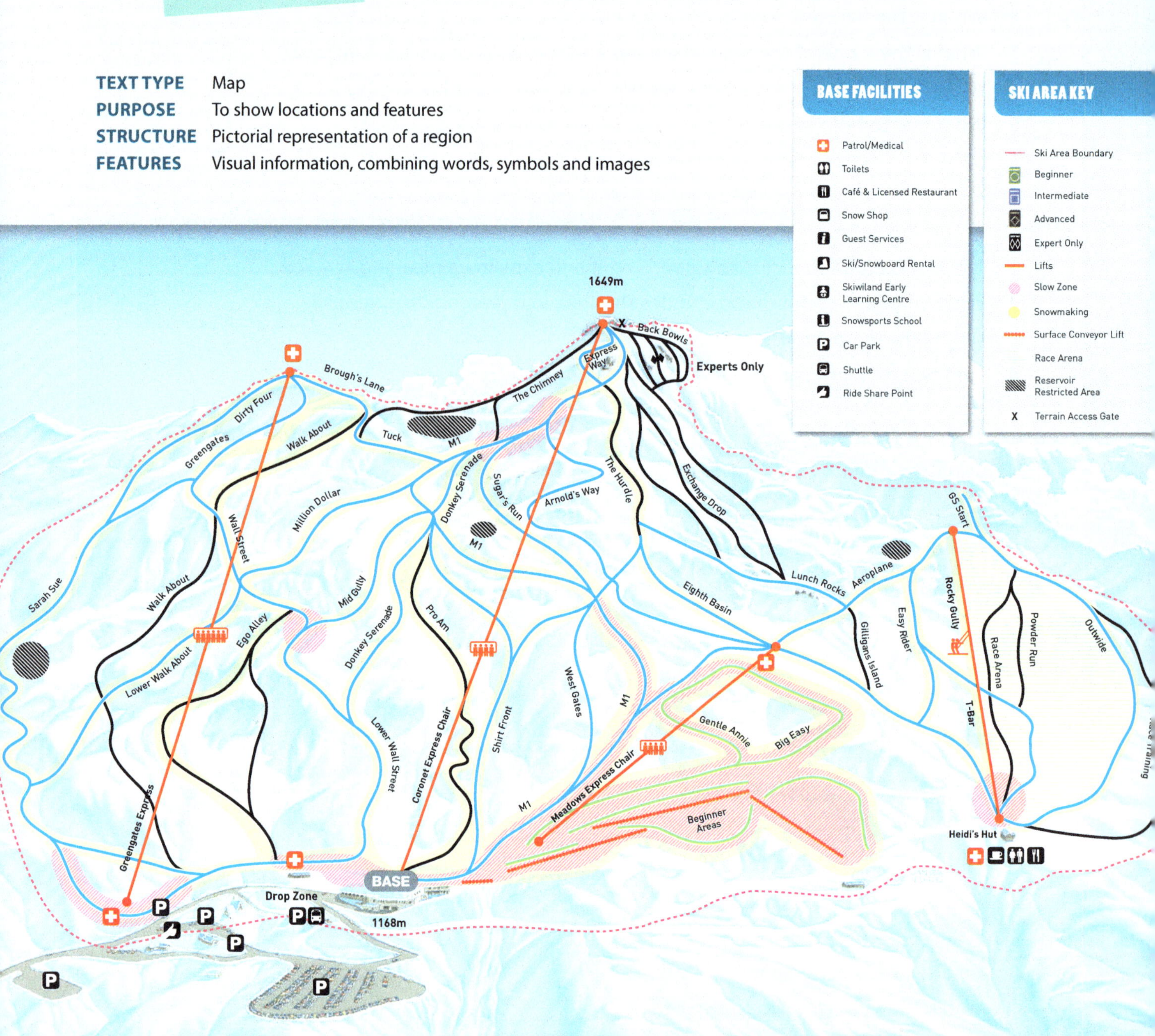

Coronet Peak is a commercial ski field in Otago, New Zealand located 18 kilometres to the northeast of the town of Queenstown and seven kilometres west of Arrowtown, on the southern slopes of the 1,649 m peak which shares its name. A popular ski resort in the southern hemisphere, Coronet Peak offers a long snow season, excellent skiing and snowboarding terrain and lift systems. The view from the ski field south across Lake Wakatipu and the smaller nearby Lake Hayes is breathtaking. Home to premier events such as the Queenstown Winter Festival and the 100% Pure New Zealand Winter Games, the après skiing is as impressive as the slopes.

ISBN 9780170260121

On the surface *(Literal comprehension – right-there questions)*

1 Coronet Peak is in which region in New Zealand?
2 Which town is closer to the Coronet Ski Field, Queenstown or Arrowtown?
3 How many medical stations are there on the ski field?
4 How many chair lifts are there on the ski field?
5 Which chairlift should you take if you wanted to ski 'The Chimney'?

Discovering techniques *(Language structures and features, spelling, grammar, vocabulary)*

This is an example of a topological map. These maps are simplified and do not always follow mapping conventions. They usually serve only one purpose.

1 What is the purpose of this map?
2 Because this is a simplified map, it has to impart information easily. This map uses a lot of symbols. Look at the Base Facilities key. There are several general symbols you could find anywhere. List them.
3 Why are different coloured lines used on the map?

Search and think *(Inferential and interpretive comprehension)*

1 Where could your little sister go if she didn't want to ski?
2 What does the red dashed line that goes around the outside of the runs represent?
3 Where would they run competitions at Coronet Peak?
4 The map suggests only a certain type of skier should ski the 'Black Bowls'. What type of skier?
5 What do you think a 'Ride Share Point' might be?
6 The lift going from Heidi's Hut is different to the other lifts. How?

Hidden depths *(Creative comprehension – responding personally, higher-order-thinking skills, making links)*

1 Using the information on this page, write some advertising copy to go on an advertisement for Coronet Peak.
2 Imagine you are an intermediate level skier. You are spending the day at Coronet Peak. You have two hours in the morning and two hours in the afternoon. Plan your day by listing the lifts and runs you will do.

Extend yourself *(Links to real life or other literature, researching, writing, creating, speaking tasks)*

1 Design a symbol for the following things you might find on a ski field but are not marked on this map:
   a Danger
   b Snowboard only area
   c Please remove your skis before entering.
2 People have had a lot of fun naming the different ski runs at Coronet Peak. Design your own ski field and have some fun of your own by creatively naming your runs.

ISBN 9780170260121

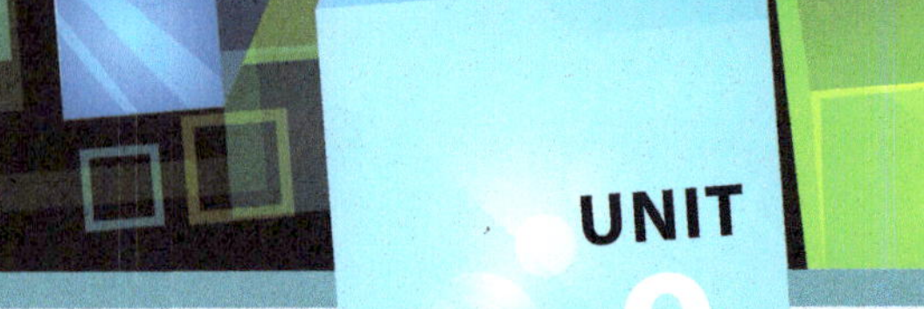

TEXT TYPE Advertisement

PURPOSE To persuade by putting forward an argument or particular point of view, to sell a product

STRUCTURE (VARIES)
1 Images
2 Written or spoken language
3 Sensory appeal – e.g. colour, shape

FEATURES May include images, facts and figures, logical reasoning, examples, and persuasive or emotive language

Blind and fighting for her life.

There is nothing sporting about bear baiting.

Every week for four years Chowti the Asiatic black bear was pitted against dogs in a brutal battle as people watched on for entertainment.

She was tied up, savagely attacked, bitten and mauled, all the time terrified and defenceless, completely blind with no idea where the next horrific dog attack would come from. Throughout Pakistan there are many bears like Chowti, brutally exploited in the cruel blood 'sport' of bear baiting and suffering constant fear and torment.

Chowti was mercifully rescued from her savage ordeal by WSPA and our local partners BRC, and is adjusting to life in the lush surroundings of the Balkasar Bear Sanctuary in Pakistan, safe and free from pain.

Please make an urgent donation today and help free bears and other animals from cruelty.

☑ **Yes, I want to help bears and other animals.**

Make an urgent donation today: ☐ $50 ☐ $100 ☐ $250 ☐ $500 or other $ ______

Title ______ First Name ______ Surname ______

Address ______ Postcode ______

Email ______ Phone ______ Mobile ______

Payment Options ☐ I enclose a personal cheque to WSPA
☐ Please charge my credit card: ☐ Visa ☐ Mastercard ☐ Diners ☐ Amex Card No. ☐☐☐☐ ☐☐☐☐ ☐☐☐☐ ☐☐☐☐

Name on card ______ Expiry ______ Signature ______

Return coupon to: WSPA New Zealand, Private Bag 93220, Parnell, Auckland 1151.

☐ Please tick this box if you would like information on how to leave WSPA in your will ☐ Please tick if you don't wish to receive information from WSPA

Thank you.

M0313A10

Call 0800 500 9772
or go to donate.wspa.org.nz/helpbears

ISBN 9780170260121

On the surface *(Literal comprehension – right-there questions)*

1 What type of bear is Chowti?
2 How many years was Chowti abused for?
3 Which country was Chowti in?
4 Which organisations rescued Chowti?
5 Where did Chowti go once she had been rescued?

Discovering techniques *(Language structures and features, spelling, grammar, vocabulary)*

1 In the orange panel, WSPA uses several emotive descriptive words to make the reader understand how badly the bear has been treated. List as many as you can.
2 Find out at least three ways that the picture of Chowti links to the words in the advertisement?

Search and think *(Inferential and interpretive comprehension)*

1 What is bear baiting?
2 Why is Chowti described as defenceless?
3 Does WSPA work to protect only bears? Find evidence from the advertisement to support your answer.
4 Why has WSPA put the word 'sport' in inverted commas?
5 How does WSPA make it easier for you to donate money?

Hidden depths *(Creative comprehension – responding personally, higher-order-thinking skills, making links)*

1 a What does WSPA stand for?
  b Give four examples of other work it is involved in besides saving bears in Pakistan.
2 There are several sports that use animals. Choose one that you think uses animals in a positive way and explain how they do this.
3 Would this advertisement encourage you to support WSPA? Why?/Why not?

Extend yourself *(Links to real life or other literature, researching, writing, creating, speaking tasks)*

1 Turn this magazine advertisement into a script for a 30-second radio advertisement. Think about sound effects, tone of voice, emphasis, pause for effect etc.
2 Your task is to encourage people of your age to donate money to an organisation of your choice. How would you do this?

ISBN 9780170260121

TEXT TYPE Magazine article
PURPOSE To inform and interest
STRUCTURE
1. Orientation – background information about who, where and when
2. Orderly explanation
3. A personal comment

FEATURES Descriptive language, facts, quotations, persuasive language

> Among all the world's oceans, the Ross Sea has been the least disturbed by human activity
>
> *SCIENCE*, 2008

The last ocean

The Ross Sea is the most pristine ocean ecosystem in the world – and the subject of international debate on whether its wildlife should be protected or whether it's fair game for restauranteurs worldwide

PHOTOGRAPHY CAMILLE SEAMAN

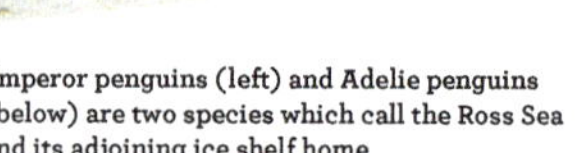

Emperor penguins (left) and Adelie penguins (below) are two species which call the Ross Sea and its adjoining ice shelf home

The Ross Sea is a large bay of Antarctica located 3,500km south of New Zealand. It hasn't substantially changed since its discovery by humans in 1841.

Fishing has the potential to transform all that. The Ross Sea is home to the Antarctic toothfish, known on high-end restaurant menus around the world as Chilean sea bass. Every year 3,000 tonne of toothfish are removed from the Ross Sea; in 20 New Zealand vessels caught 70 tonnes at an expo value of $20 million.

Concerned this could unbalance the Ross Sea's unspoilt ecosystem, activist groups are campaigning for it to become a Marine Protected Area (MPA) where fishing is prohibited.

As the award-winning Kiwi doco *The Last Ocean* revealed, the Antarctic toothfish might be an ugly chap, but he lives for up to 50 years and reproduces later in life - meaning he's highly vulnerable to overfishing. As numbers drop, so do those of species who eat toothfish for lunch, such as Weddell seals and Ross Sea killer whales.

In November 2012, the 25 member countries of the Convention for the Conservation of Antarctic Marine Living Resources (CCAMLR) couldn't reach a consensus on how to protect the Ross Sea. The next meeting is in July 2013.

Last Ocean director Peter Young wasn't surprised by CCAMLR's failure to agree. "We knew it wasn't going to be a quick fix when you're dealing with an international issue like this. Even though it was a little disappointing."

But the longer the debate continues, Peter points out, the more impact we'll have on the Ross Sea. All for the sake of a marginal fishery and a posh menu fixture? "We don't need to be there," he says. "Nothing makes sense about it. It's a dangerous place to fish - it poses huge risk to human life and to the environment."

You can get involved at www.lastocean.org

ISBN 9780170260121

On the surface *(Literal comprehension – right-there questions)*

1 Where is the Ross Sea?

2 What fish is found in the Ross Sea?

3 What is another name for the Antarctic toothfish?

4 How long does the Antarctic toothfish live for?

5 Name two species of penguin that call the Ross Sea home.

Optional Assessment: 5 x 1 mark = 5 marks

Discovering techniques *(Language structures and features, spelling, grammar, vocabulary)*

1 What do the following letters stand for?

   a MPA

   b CCAMLR

2 Find examples of colloquial language that are used in this article.

3 Find the superlative in the subheading of this article.

Optional Assessment: 3 x 1 mark = 3 marks

Search and think *(Inferential and interpretive comprehension)*

1 Why is the Antarctic Toothfish vulnerable to overfishing?

2 The members of the Convention for the Conservation of Antarctic Marine Living Resources (CCAMLR) couldn't reach a consensus on how to protect the Ross Sea. What is does this mean?

3 The article is called 'The Last Ocean'. Give the two meanings of this phrase.

4 Think about why it would pose 'huge risk to human life' to fish in the Ross Sea? Research some details that support your thoughts.

5 What was the author hoping to achieve by putting the website at the end of the article?

Optional Assessment: 5 x 1 mark = 5 marks

Hidden depths *(Creative comprehension – responding personally, higher-order-thinking skills, making links)*

1 Imagine you are taking part in a debate with the moot 'That the environment is more important than the dollar'. Pick which team you would be on (Affirmative or Negative) and that you are speaker one. Write the introduction of your speech.

2 Can you explain why the article is surrounded by photos of penguins and not toothfish?

3 Draw a map of Antarctica and on it mark the Ross Sea.

Extend yourself *(Links to real life or other literature, researching, writing, creating, speaking tasks)*

1 Find out if there was any change to this issue after the July 2013 meeting mentioned in this article.

2 This article outlines an 'international debate' on whether wildlife should be protected or whether it's 'fair game'. Research another animal that is under a similar threat to the Antarctic Toothfish.

ISBN 9780170260121

UNIT 11

TEXT TYPE	Advertisement
PURPOSE	To persuade by putting forward an argument or particular point of view, to sell a product
STRUCTURE (VARIES)	1 Images 2 Written or spoken language 3 Sensory appeal – e.g. colour, shape
FEATURES	May include images, facts and figures, logical reasoning, examples, and persuasive or emotive language

On the surface *(Literal comprehension – right-there questions)*

1 What is the name of the:
   a company that makes the bread?
   b brand of the bread?
   c variety of the bread?
2 What is the slogan for this product?
3 What is a 'damson'?
4 What month does Margie Chambers pick the fruit?
5 Where does the advertisement tell you to go for more information on Two Hands bread?

Discovering techniques *(Language structures and features, spelling, grammar, vocabulary)*

1 Use a dictionary to find the meanings of the following words as they are used in the text:
   a renders
   b alchemy
   c diminutive
   d compromise
   e artisanal.
2 Find three examples of alliteration from the body copy (main text).
3 Write down the compound word used in the advertisement.

Search and think *(Inferential and interpretive comprehension)*

1 What does the word 'puckering' suggest?
2 Does Margie make the bread?
3 Why is Margie's story in this advertisement?
4 What does the concept of something being 'hand-made' suggest?
5 Why have a photograph of the actual packaged loaf of bread?

Hidden depths *(Creative comprehension – responding personally, higher-order-thinking skills, making links)*

1 Look carefully at the photograph of the table. How does it reinforce the concept of hand-made and taking time to enjoy quality food?
2 Advertising is everywhere you look. Sometimes subtle, sometimes very obvious. Explain what advertising you stop and take in. Find an example.

Extend yourself *(Links to real life or other literature, researching, writing, creating, speaking tasks)*

1 Create your own brand of bread and write the body copy for an advertisement.
   Think about:
   - the product you are going to sell (brown, white, high fibre, natural ...)
   - your market (old, young, mothers ...)
   - the angle you are going to take
   - what language techniques you will use to sell your product (adjectives, emotive language ...)
2 Find another advertisement for bread. What do they have in common? What is different? Think about language, layout, style.

ISBN 9780170260121

UNIT 12

TEXT TYPE Explanation

PURPOSE To inform, to explain how or why things are as they are, or how things work

STRUCTURE
1. A general statement
2. Series of statement or events in chronological or logical order
3. Concluding statement

FEATURES Logical sequence of details or ideas may use heading, diagrams and tables

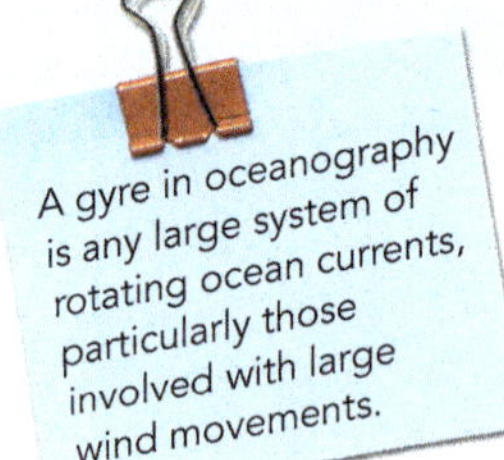

A gyre in oceanography is any large system of rotating ocean currents, particularly those involved with large wind movements.

THE GREAT PACIFIC GARBAGE PATCH

The Great Pacific Garbage Patch, also described as the 'Pacific Trash Vortex', is a gyre of marine debris in the central North Pacific Ocean.

It is thought that the Great Pacific Garbage Patch formed gradually as a result of marine pollution gathered by oceanic currents. The gyre's rotational pattern draws in waste material from across the North Pacific Ocean, including coastal waters off North America and Japan. As material is captured in the currents, wind-driven surface currents gradually move floating debris toward the centre, trapping it in the region.

It is estimated 80% of the garbage comes from land-based sources and 20% from ships. Ship-generated pollution is a source of concern, since a typical 3,000 passenger cruise ship produces over eight tonnes of solid waste weekly, a major amount of which ends up in the patch, as most of the waste is organic. Pollutants range in size from abandoned fishing nets to plastic micro-pellets used in abrasive cleaners. Currents carry debris from the west coast of North America to the gyre in about six years, and debris from the east coast of Asia in a year or less.

It is likely that the land-based sources of pollutants and plastics come from the great rivers from around the world. The Ganges, in India, is an example of a source of major sea pollution. Others include the major rivers of Bangladesh, Nigeria, and other developing nations.

ESTIMATES OF SIZE

The size of the patch is unknown, as large items readily visible from a boat deck are uncommon. The patch is not easily visible because it consists of very small pieces, almost invisible to the naked eye, and most of its contents are suspended beneath the surface of the ocean. A similar patch of floating plastic debris is found in the Atlantic Ocean.

EFFECT ON WILDLIFE

Midway Atoll receives twenty tonnes of marine debris from the patch. Of the 1.5 million Laysan Albatrosses that inhabit Midway, nearly all are found to have plastic in their digestive system. Approximately one-third of the chicks die as their parents confuse brightly coloured plastic with marine animals (such as squid and fish) for food. Because albatross chicks do not develop the reflex to regurgitate until they are four months old, they cannot expel the plastic pieces. Albatrosses are not the only species to suffer from the plastic pollution; sea turtles and monk seals also consume the debris. All kinds of plastic items wash upon the shores, from cigarette lighters to toothbrushes and toys. An albatross on Midway can have up to 50% of its intestinal tract filled with plastic.

On the surface *(Literal comprehension – right-there questions)*

1. What is another name for the Great Pacific Garbage Patch?
2. How long does it take for debris from the east coast of Asia to reach the Great Pacific Garbage Patch gyre?
3. Why is it impossible to detect the size of the Great Pacific Garbage Patch?
4. Where is a similar patch of floating plastic debris found?
5. Name the two marine animals this passage specifically mentions as being affected by the Great Pacfic Garbage Patch.
6. How much plastic debris washes up on Midway Atoll every year?

Discovering techniques *(Language structures and features, spelling, grammar, vocabulary)*

1. List the verbs in paragraph two that are chosen to show how the gyre accumulates waste.
2. This piece contains both facts and opinions. Which words begin paragraphs that contain opinions?
3. Why are the words 'squid' and 'fish' in brackets?

Search and think *(Inferential and interpretive comprehension)*

1. What is the tone of this passage? Do you think the writer has an opinion about the gyre?
2. Why do approximately one-third of the Laysan Albatross chicks that inhabit Midway die?
3. How is it that the plastic debris kills the sea birds and turtles?

Hidden depths *(Creative comprehension – responding personally, higher-order-thinking skills, making links)*

1. Find a map of the the Great Pacific Garbage Patch.
2. Find five more key facts about the the Great Pacific Garbage Patch.
3. Where does your home's rubbish end up? Find out.
4. What do you think individual humans can do to help this problem?

Extend yourself *(Links to real life or other literature, researching, writing, creating, speaking tasks)*

1. Plastic bags are also a cause for many sea turtle deaths. Research why this is the case.
2. Write a speech with the title 'Recycle – save the planet'.
3. Research Midway Atoll. Present the information you find as a poster.
4. If you live near a beach, go and see what rubbish is accumulating there. Record your findings.

ISBN 9780170260121

UNIT 13

Herald reporter Jamie Morton tackles the challenge of eating the Jumbo Beef Burger from Angelo's Pizza in Waihi. Photo / Christine Cornege.

TEXT TYPE Newspaper article

PURPOSE To persuade by putting forward an argument or particular point of view

STRUCTURE
1 Point of view stated
2 Justifications of argument in a logical order
3 Summing up of argument

FEATURES Facts and figures, logical reasoning, examples, persuasive or emotive language

WAIHI BEACH SHOP MANAGERS RECKON THEY MAY MAKE COUNTRY'S BIGGEST HAMBURGER

By Jamie Morton Monday Jan 21, 2013

They've created a monster. But few who order the Jumbo Burger from Waihi Beach's Angelo's Pizzas know what they're getting themselves in for until the behemoth stack of meat, bread and veges is presented to them on a large plate that barely contains it.

Weighing in at 1.5kg, the brute burger towers so high above a regular Big Mac that, when placed next to the brute, McDonald's most celebrated icon simply appears as a newborn at its mother's side.

It's a question store managers Corry and Annelie Joubert have been asked countless times, and have often wondered themselves – could this be New Zealand's biggest hamburger?

'I've never seen one bigger ... and we've been around a lot,' Mrs Joubert said.

Unsurprisingly, the inspiration for their giant burger came a few years ago from the home of everything super-sized, the United States.

'We got an email from someone about an American place where they had this massive burger ... so we thought we should try and make that burger ourselves.'

They then hit the first hurdle – where to get buns big enough. Their local bakery solved the problem, fashioning a prototype about three times as wide as even the largest available at most takeaway shops.

Measuring 19cm across, the bun itself is enough to scare off many customers who ask the Jouberts exactly what they mean by Jumbo.

What goes inbetween reads like a typical family grocery shopping list - half a lettuce, a whole chopped tomato, three fried eggs, two large slices of shoulder bacon, three or four gherkins, a quarter of an onion, mustard, tomato sauce and a special cheese sauce that flows down the sides of the beast.

The burgers are two 180g patties that, as hefty as they are, are placed alongside each other rather than stacked. One of its patties constitutes 30.6g of fat – nearly 5g more than that of an entire Big Mac.

Carl Nelson holds the honour of being the first person to eat the entire stack. He was a teenager working at the store at the time and accepted a challenge that he wouldn't be charged if he could finish the heap in one sitting.

Over the busy summer season, the shop sells about 10 of the $19.95 burgers each week, and Mrs Joubert guessed only about every one in two customers could finish one.

'It's not a big seller, just mainly a fun thing, and it's all mainly big guys who order it,' she said.

The record for the biggest burger commercially available goes to Juicy's Outlaw Grill in Corvallis, Oregon, for a burger weighing 352.44kg, which costs $6000 and demands 48 hours' notice to prepare.

By the numbers

McDonald's Big Mac

Price:	$5.60
Weight:	195g
Fat:	25.9g
Saturated Fat:	4.8g

Burger King Whopper

Price:	$6.80
Fat:	36.8g
Saturated Fat:	11.3g

Angelo's Pizzas Jumbo Beef Burger

Price:	$19.95
Weight:	1.5kg
Fat in one meat pattie:	30.6g
Saturated fat (in one meat pattie):	15.3g
Probable fat: Well over	100g

  ISBN 9780170260121

On the surface *(Literal comprehension – right-there questions)*

1 Where is Angelo's Pizza located?
2 What is the name of the burger that this article describes?
3 How much does this burger weigh?
4 What is unique about the bun of this burger?
5 How much does it cost?

Discovering techniques *(Language structures and features, spelling, grammar, vocabulary)*

1 Which language feature is found in the headline of this article?
2 What language feature is found in the first sentence of this article?
3 Use a dictionary to find the meanings of the following words as they are used in the text.
   a behemoth
   b icon
   c prototype.

Search and think *(Inferential and interpretive comprehension)*

1 Write the shopping list to create this burger.
2 When are most of the burgers sold?
3 Why did Carl Nelson attempt to eat the burger?
4 Are the patties in the Jumbo Burger more or less fatty then the Big Mac?
5 What does the photograph add to the article?
6 What could be another name for the Jumbo Burger?

Hidden depths *(Creative comprehension – responding personally, higher-order-thinking skills, making links)*

1 Imagine you were given a challenge to eat a Jumbo Burger. Write the 'story' of your attempt to overcome it. Remember to use all the five senses in your description.
2 A newspaper article should give you the 5W's: Who? What? Where? Why? When? Find the information that answers these five questions in the article.

Who?	
What?	
Where?	
Why?	
When?	

3 Design your own burger. Be creative!

Extend yourself *(Links to real life or other literature, researching, writing, creating, speaking tasks)*

1 Is the Jumbo Burger good food? Explain your response.
2 Design an advertisement for the Jumbo Burger.
3 The article says the United States is the 'home of everything super-sized'. What does this mean? Find out.

TEXT TYPE Dictionary

PURPOSE To give the meaning, pronunciation, grammatical use and history of words in a language

STRUCTURE
1 Head word
2 Definitions
3 Usage
4 Explanation

FEATURES Alphabetical order, punctuation, font changes

In this exercise, the dictionary is one that lists well-known phrases and fables rather than words.

Break. In addition to the phrases below, the expressions 'to get a break' and 'to make a break' are used colloquially in different ways. To get a break means to be offered an unexpected chance or to have an opportunity of advancing oneself. To make a break can mean either to make a complete change in one's life, either temporarily (as from a holiday) or more permanently (as through a change in occupation), or to run up a score in billiards or snooker.

Break, To. To bankrupt. Hence broke to mean penniless.

Also, of a boy's voice, to 'crack' or alter at puberty. The reference here may be to a bell, whose 'voice' alters if it is cracked.

Break a butterfly on a wheel, To. To employ great effort in the accomplishment of a small matter.

Satire or sense, alas! Can Sporus feel?
Who breaks a butterfly upon the wheel?
ALEXANDER POPE: *Epistle to Dr Arbuthnot (1735)*

Break flag, To. To hoist it rolled up and to 'break it, or let it fly, by pulling the halyard to release the hitch that holds it together.

Break a journey, To. To stop before the journey is accomplished, with the intention of completing it later.

Break a promise, To. To go back on one's word.

Break away, To. To escape; to go off abruptly.

Break camp, To. To pack up camping equipment and leave.

Break cover, To. To emerge suddenly from a hiding place; of a hunted animal or person, to come out of a covert or hiding place. The den of a fox is usually blocked the night before a hunt so that it is obliged to seek some other cover. When it leaves that cover, the hunt is on.

Break down, To. To cease to function; to collapse. A nervous breakdown is a mental illness in which the patient ceases to function properly.

Breakers ahead. Hidden danger is at hand. Breakers in an open sea are a sign of sunken rocks, sandbanks or other submerged obstacles.

Break even, To. To reach the point in a financial activity, whether gambling or commercial, at which one makes neither profit not loss.

Break in, To. To interrupt a conversation with a remark of one's own; to accustom a person or animal to a particular way of life or routine; to enter a building with the aim of stealing or committing some other crime. Breaking and entering was the former legal term for the act of doing this.

Breaking of bread, To. The EUCHARIST. In scriptural language to break bread is to share food with others.

Break new ground, To. To do something that has not been done before. The allusion is probably to digging a new trench in a siege operation or to commence a new project, as a settler does in a new country.

Break off, To. To stop working; to conclude a conversation; to end an engagement or friendship.

Break one's back, To. To overwork or work very hard. The metaphor is from carrying burdens on the back.

Break one's duck, To. To score one's first run in a CRICKET match. See also DUCK'S EGG.

Break one's fast, To. To take food after long abstinence. Hence breakfast after the night's fast.

Break one's heart, To. To pine away or die of disappointment. To be brokenhearted is to be overwhelmed by grief or disappointment. It is possible to die 'of a broken heart'.

Break one's neck, To. To dislocate the bones of one's neck; to do something energetically at great speed; to be in a great and possibly dangerous hurry.

Break on the wheel, To. To torture on a 'wheel' by breaking the bones of the body with an iron bar. See also COUP DE GRACE.

Break out, To. To escape from prison; to throw off restraint.

Break serve, To. In tennis to win a game in which one's opponent is serving.

Break ship, To. Of a sailor, to fail to return to one's ship on the expiration of leave.

Break someone's heart, To. To make someone grieve or feel very acute distress, especially through love.

Break the back of, To. To complete the greatest or hardest part of a difficult task.

Break the bank, To. To ruin financially, especially through a successful gambling move.

Break the enemy's line, To. To create a gap in his ORDER OF BATTLE (As Nelson did at Trafalgar and Wellington did at Salamanca), and so put him to confusion.

Break the ice, To. To be the first to do something; to dispel the stiffness and reserve of a first meeting or conversation.

Break the mould, To. To change from one's usual habits.

Break the news, To. To be the first to give it to someone, often delicately or tactfully.

Break through, To. To force a passage; to overcome major obstacles, especially in the field of scientific or technical progress.

Break up, To. To break into pieces; to smash; to finish classes at the end of term and go home; to separate or disperse.

Break wind, To. To emit intestinal gas from the anus.

Break with, To. To end an association or relationship. A break with tradition is a change from customary procedure.

  ISBN 9780170260121

On the surface *(Literal comprehension – right-there questions)*

1 How many phrases using the word 'Break' are listed?

2 In your own words, explain what it means 'to break flag'.

3 What is Epistle to Dr Arbuthnot (1735)?

4 The phrase 'To Break one's duck' is connected to which sport?

Discovering techniques *(Language structures and features, spelling, grammar, vocabulary)*

1 Why are some words in capital letters?

2 An allusion is suggested for one phrase. Which one? What is the allusion?

3 Why are brackets used in 'Break the enemy's lines, To'. Which other entry could have used brackets in a similar way?

Search and think *(Inferential and interpretive comprehension)*

1 Why is each entry written with the second word first?

2 Which phrase is based on which former legal term? Explain the term.

3 Which one of these phrases would you use if you were explaining a day of very hard work?

4 Which phrase means to come out of hiding?

5 Choose one phrase that has a literal meaning connected with the human body and a figurative meaning. Explain the connection in your own words

Hidden depths *(Creative comprehension – responding personally, higher-order-thinking skills, making links)*

1 Explain where the following words come from:
   - breakfast
   - heartbroken
   - breakthrough.

2 Choose two examples that link the word 'break' with the word 'wheel'. Explain how the literal meaning has led to the metaphorical meaning.

3 Write a conversation between two people that uses as many of these phrases as you can. Remember that it needs to make sense!

Extend yourself *(Links to real life or other literature, researching, writing, creating, speaking tasks)*

1 Choose another word in English that has many phrases built upon it. List as many as you and your friends can think of.

2 Choose at least three of these phrases and find examples of how they have been used in real life. The Internet makes this easy.

UNIT 15

TEXT TYPE Book review

PURPOSE To give details and opinion on a text

STRUCTURE
1. Context – background information on the text.
   Details of author (other texts, prizes, etc.)
2. Description of the text (including characters and plot)
3. Intended audience
4. Concluding statement (judgement, opinion or recommendation)

FEATURES Language may be formal or informal depending on purpose and audience, may include examples and quotes, publisher and price

Contact | Blog

Gone by Michael Grant

In the blink of an eye. Everyone disappears. GONE.

I read *Gone* several years ago, back when it was the only instalment in Michael Grant's collection of quasi-dystopian, young adult literature. By the time that I realised that there were sequels out, four more books had been published and I suddenly found myself far behind. Consequently, I recently decided that it was time that I caught up with the kids of Perdido Beach and their many problems, and so I picked up *Gone* with the intention of reading all five of the series' instalments before the conclusive *Light* is released later this year.

Truth be told, I was worried when I started this book. I remember liking it a lot when I first read it all that time ago, but I was also mindful of the fact that I hadn't been a very thorough reader then. Thankfully, however, *Gone* manages to be just about as good as I remember. Sure, there are some things that irk me, but what Grant does right far outshines the little issues, and that makes this book worthwhile, despite its flaws.

GONE
MICHAEL GRANT

Michael Grant is ridiculously creative, and this little fact automatically makes this book a shining beacon in a genre that tends to tell the same stories over and over again. It doesn't waste any time jumping right into the crazy, with our protagonist witnessing the sudden and inexplicable disappearance of his teacher on the very first page, and doesn't let up once. Grant throws out new mysteries and developments at a rapid pace, quickly turning what starts out as a relatively straightforward story into a complex and mind-bending experience. New ideas are constantly introduced, while ones that you thought you understood obtain twists that leave you, once more, confused and unsure. Kids develop supernatural abilities. Animals start mutating. I could go on, but I wouldn't want to ruin any of the fun.

We don't get any of the usual YA silliness here. No love triangles. No predictable turns that are passed off as surprising, despite their complete lack of subtlety or originality. Grant continually pulls out genuine surprises.

Because of this, *Gone* never settles on a uniform tone, and this is an entirely wonderful thing. It has everything that you could possibly want from a YA book because of it. Moments of genuine humour that are laugh-out-loud funny. Moments of touching emotion. Moments of dark maturity that are shocking and profound, due to the fact that these instances of cruelty and sadness solely involve children.

Grant's writing style, though a bit shaky and not without its problems, is tight and altogether clever. It's simple and easy to read, but has plenty of depth as well, thanks to its more poetic moments. The dialogue is the highlight here, providing the majority of the humour and heart. It reads a bit oddly at times, but this is easy to accept, given that the speakers are all in their early teens, if that. In fact, the grammatical incorrectness of much of the dialogue actually lends a good deal of realism to the characters who speak it.

Bottom line? *Gone*'s world is bizarre, unorthodox, and altogether packed with awesome.

Grant's first instalment in his defining series is all-round fantastic, and far better than most of the drivel that passes for contemporary YA. I get the feeling that this will be one of those works that only improves. As a result, I now eagerly turn to *Hunger* for the next chapter of this tale. Bravo, Grant. Bravo.

The Score So Far

I'll be keeping a running list of the series as I read, in which I rank each instalment from best to worst. Which book will take the number one spot in the end? Place your bets!

1. *Gone* 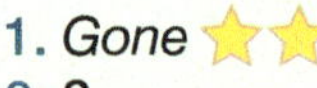
2. ?
3. ?
4. ?
5. ?

ISBN 9780170260121

On the surface *(Literal comprehension – right-there questions)*

1 What sort of novel is being reviewed here?
2 Who wrote the novel?
3 How many novels are there in the whole series?
4 Where is the novel set?
5 How many stars did the book get?

Discovering techniques *(Language structures and features, spelling, grammar, vocabulary)*

1 Use a dictionary to find the meaning of the following words as they are used in the text:
   a dystopian
   b quasi-dystopian
   c irk
   d drivel
   e bravo.
2 Copy the metaphor that the reviewer has used to describe this novel.
3 Reviewers use positive and negative descriptive words. List the positive words/phrases that have been used to describe the book.
4 The reviewer thinks that the dialogue is both a highlight and a lowlight of the book. Give the reasons why he/she thinks this.

Search and think *(Inferential and interpretive comprehension)*

1 What is the title of the second novel in the series?
2 When did the reviewer read the novel?
3 What worried the reviewer about going back to reread the novel?
4 The reviewer obviously doesn't always like young adult fiction. What does the reviewer have a problem with?
5 How does the reviewer make the review sound as if he/she is chatting to his reader?

Hidden depths *(Creative comprehension – responding personally, higher-order-thinking skills, making links)*

1 Using the Internet, download and print a copy of a review for a book you have read recently. Use different coloured highlighters to show:
   - Facts
   - Reviewer's opinion
   - Positive words/phrases
   - Negative words/phrases.
2 What do you think about reading a book for a second time? Is it a good idea? Which novels have you read more than once?
3 What other dystopian novels or films do you know? Create a list.

Extend yourself *(Links to real life or other literature, researching, writing, creating, speaking tasks)*

1 Read the novel *Gone*. Write a review of it yourself.
2 Read the other books in the series.
3 Write a scene from a story based in a dystopian time.
4 Reread a series of novels you read and enjoyed when you were a bit younger. What do you think about it now? Has your reader's eye developed? Explain.

ISBN 9780170260121

UNIT 16

TEXT TYPE Editorial

PURPOSE To persuade by offering a particular point of view

STRUCTURE
1 Topic outlined
2 Justification of argument in a logical order
3 Summing up of argument
4 The newspaper's opinion

FEATURES Persuasive language, logical reasoning, examples, facts and figures

Hobbit's LA premiere still a winner for NZ

Fans upset red carpet won't roll out again in Wellington.

The new Hobbit movie will get the traditional Hollywood-style premiere in Los Angeles.

In the week that Warner Bros released the first teaser-trailer of *The Hobbit: The Desolation of Smaug*, some New Zealanders were disappointed to learn that the premiere on December 13 will not take place in Wellington.

There will be no repeat of the day last November when 100,000 fans lined the red carpet and a specially adorned Air New Zealand plane flew overhead as the first of *The Hobbit* trilogy was launched.

Instead, the new movie will get the traditional Hollywood-style premiere in Los Angeles.

The disappointment is understandable. November 28, 2012, will always be remembered as a special day for the local movie industry, Wellington and the country.

Further, it might have been assumed the very generous tax breaks handed to Warner Bros to film the trilogy here carried some sort of obligation to hold the premiere in the capital. In reality, however, there is little reason to complain.

Using LA will mean the premiere will lose much of its uniqueness. It will be just one of the many films launched there each month.

That aside, there are obvious advantages in highlighting the film in the very centre of the movie industry. There will also be no loss to New Zealand in terms of the film's impact. International audiences will still associate it with this country.

Some, encouraged further by Tourism New Zealand marketing, will see it as a reason to visit. Therein lies the film's real value.

Editor Jeremy Rees

Letters to the editor
letters@nzherald.co.nz

News contacts
newsdesk@herald.co.nz

Postal address
PO Box 32, Auckland

Street address
46 Albert St, Auckland
Phone (09) 379 5050. Fax (09) 373-6406

On the surface *(Literal comprehension – right-there questions)*

1 What does the abbreviation 'LA' stand for?
2 When and where will the premiere take place?
3 How many people watched the people arrive for the first Hobbit movie premiere? Where?
4 For which groups was that first Hobbit premiere a special event?
5 How many ways have they given for you to contact the newspaper?

Discovering techniques *(Language structures and features, spelling, grammar, vocabulary)*

1 Comment on the use of the phrase 'red carpet'. It is used in two senses. Explain them both.
2 Find the example of alliteration in the Editorial.
3 In a dictionary, look up the word 'premiere'. Where does it originate?
4 Why is there a colon in the title of the film?

Search and think *(Inferential and interpretive comprehension)*

1 What does the phrase 'specially adorned' mean?
2 What does the Editorial suggest are the negatives of a Hollywood-style premiere?
3 Why does the Editorial suggest Warner Brothers should feel obliged to hold the premiere in Wellington?
4 What does the Editorial suggest is the real value of the film to New Zealand?

Hidden depths *(Creative comprehension – responding personally, higher-order-thinking skills, making links)*

1 An Editorial offers an opinion. Whose opinion? About what? What is its purpose?
2 How does this Editorial shape its opinion?

Extend yourself *(Links to real life or other literature, researching, writing, creating, speaking tasks)*

1 Find newspaper articles describing the first Hobbit premiere
2 Find an image of the Air New Zealand plane in its special Hobbit livery. Design a similar paint job for a plane using another well-known New Zealand icon.
3 Write a letter to the Editor, challenging the ideas expressed in this Editorial.
4 Write a fictional account of attending the first Hobbit premiere as an actor in the movie.

UNIT 17

TEXT TYPE Explanation
PURPOSE To inform, to explain how or why things are as they are, or how things work
STRUCTURE
1 A general statement
2 Series of statement or events in chronological or logical order
3 Concluding statement

FEATURES Logical sequence of details or ideas may use heading, diagrams and tables

Fractures and dislocations

A dislocation is where a bone has been displaced from its normal position at a joint. A fracture is when a bone has been broken.

Fractures

A fracture is termed:

- closed where there is no break in the skin;
- open where the bone end has broken the skin or a wound is present with the fracture.

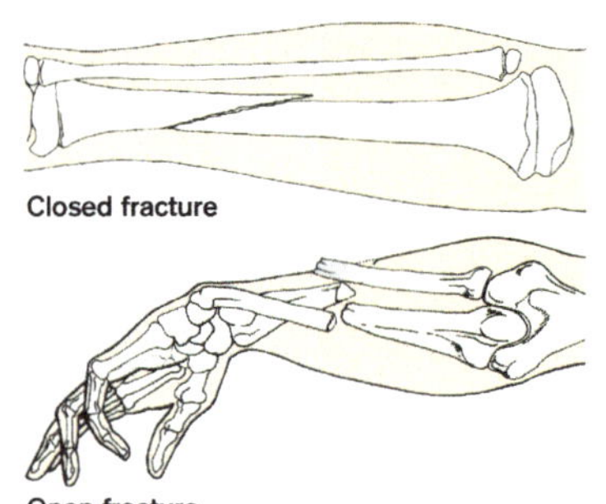
Closed fracture
Open fracture

The fractured or dislocated part should not be moved and first aid should be confined to providing soft padding and support in the position chosen by the patient.

In a remote area, or where ambulance or medical care is likely to be delayed for an hour or more, the first aider may use simple immobilisation techniques to reduce pain and spasm. In such cases it is the first aider's responsibility to monitor the circulation in any affected limb to ensure that the immobilisation has not stopped blood flow or affected the nerve supply to an extremity.

Dislocations

Symptoms and signs – not all may be present

- Pain
- Swelling

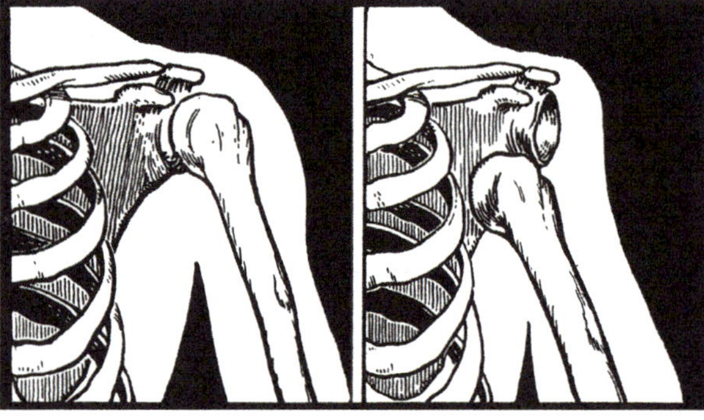

- Deformity of the injured area (when compared with the uninjured side of the body)
- Loss of normal function of the injured part
- Discolouration of the skin (i.e. blueness) or bruising
- A wound if it is an open fracture
- Altered sensation – e.g. 'pins and needles' – if a nerve is under pressure
- A grating sensation if injured bone ends are rubbing together
- Patient may have heard/felt the bone break.

How you can help

1. Control any bleeding
   - If a wound is present, check for any significant bleeding; and if bleeding, apply direct pressure around any exposed bones.
   - Apply padding around the wound, or above and below the wound. Apply a clean dressing loosely over the injured part.

Call 111 for an ambulance.

2. Immobilise the injured part
   - Reduce the pain and the risk of further injury by supporting and immobilising the injured area. Usually this simply means supporting the injured part in a comfortable position.
3. Make the patient comfortable
   - Help the patient into the position of greatest comfort without any unnecessary movement. Use blankets, pillows or clothing for general comfort and support.
   - Place generous padding around the injured area and in the nearby hollows of the body, using soft towels, clothing, pillows or blankets, etc.
   - Where an ambulance is likely to be delayed for more than 1 hour immobilise the injured part. Specific immobilisation techniques for various injuries are outlined on the following pages.

DO NOT move the patient or any injured part unnecessarily.

ISBN 9780170260121

On the surface *(Literal comprehension – right-there questions)*

1 What is the difference between a fracture and a dislocation?
2 What are the two ways to categorise a fracture?
3 If an ambulance or medical care is likely to be delayed for more than an hour, what should the first aider do?
4 What three main things can a first aider do to help the injured person?
5 If a wound is present, what does a first aider need to check for?

Discovering techniques *(Language structures and features, spelling, grammar, vocabulary)*

1 How does the writer change the topic of 'first aid' into the title of the person being advised?
2 What do you notice about the way the written information has been set out on the page? Why has this technique been used?
3 Select three words that instruct the reader. (Imperatives/commands)
4 There is an example of onomatopoeia in the piece. What is it? Why is it used?
5 Why are some of the words in capital letters?

Search and think *(Inferential and interpretive comprehension)*

1 What is the difference between 'i.e.' and 'e.g.' as used in this piece?
2 Think about the sentence structure of this piece. What do you notice about it?
3 How can you tell there is further information to read on this topic?
4 Why have diagrams been included in this piece?

Hidden depths *(Creative comprehension – responding personally, higher-order-thinking skills, making links)*

1 After reading these instructions, would you feel confident in helping someone with a fracture or dislocation? What else would you need? Give your reasons.
2 How important is it for a person of your age to know basic first aid? Explain.

Extend yourself *(Links to real life or other literature, researching, writing, creating, speaking tasks)*

1 Research the history of the Order of St John.
2 Research the role of a St John Youth Cadet.
3 Talk to someone who has suffered from a dislocation or fracture. Go through the Order of St John instructions with them and ask if they reflect their personal experience. Record their answer.
4 Create an instruction page for something you know how to do.

ISBN 9780170260121

TEXT TYPE Poem
PURPOSE To express ideas in precise and powerful language
STRUCTURE Lines, rhyme, rhythm, verses
FEATURES Careful word choice for meaning and sound, figurative language, verse, rhyme, imagery

The Last Wolf Speaks from the Zoo

By day
I hid in the ferns
pressed to the earth,
dressed in a coat
brown as turf.
Sunlight warmed
the patches where
my wolf pack once lay.

Day after day
childflesh spills past the wire;
they pause, point and stare –
I size them up –
glare back –
through thin red eyes.

Years back
my sister caught one –
cracked a finger –
left the childflesh
to scowl and howl.

The next day
they took my sister away.
But her smell stayed
trapped in the earth's spoor.
It took a full moon's span
for it to fade.

Now, alone,
I watch
and wait for her.

At night
the stars glisten.
I listen for the pack,
I sing to the moon.
I croon an ancient tune,
But she is muzzled
And cannot answer back.

By Pie Corbett

  ISBN 9780170260121

On the surface *(Literal comprehension – right-there questions)*

1 How many wolves are in the exhibit?
2 What is 'childflesh'?
3 Why did they take the wolf's 'sister' away?
4 How long is a full moon's span?
5 What does the wolf 'watch and wait for'?

Discovering techniques *(Language structures and features, spelling, grammar, vocabulary)*

1 Use a dictionary to find the meanings of the following words as they are used in the text:
   a turf   b spoor
   c span   d croon.
2 Find an example of each of the following poetic techniques in the poem.
   a Simile   b Metaphor   c Personification
   d Alliteration   e Onomatopoeia

Search and think *(Inferential and interpretive comprehension)*

1 How do you know that this wolf wasn't the only wolf to have been in this enclosure?
2 Who do you think the 'they' is in the following lines?

   The next day
   they took my sister away.

3 Why do you imagine a wolf would measure the length of time his sister had been gone by the moon?
4 Do you think the wolf likes being in the zoo? Explain your answer with details from the poem.
5 The last verse is about sound. What is the sound saying about the wolf's emotions?
6 Do you think the sister of the wolf was unjustly punished?

Hidden depths *(Creative comprehension – responding personally, higher-order-thinking skills, making links)*

1 Zoos have changed a lot in the last 50 years. Research a modern zoo and explain how they are trying to develop more natural habitats for animals.
2 Do you believe that zoos should be abolished? Give three reasons to support your answer.
3 Zoos have 'description panels' outside exhibits to teach the visitors about the animals. Write the description that would be in front of this wolf's exhibit. Think about both the basic facts and other details that might interest visitors.

Extend yourself *(Links to real life or other literature, researching, writing, creating, speaking tasks)*

1 Find another poem that has 'animal/s in the zoo' as a theme, whether it be positive or negative. Compare the poet's thoughts to the ideas expressed in this poem.
2 Write a poem or a description of another sort of animal in a zoo.
3 Write a poem or a description of how a wolf lives in the wild.

UNIT 19

TEXT TYPE Recount

PURPOSE To reconstruct past experiences by retelling events in the order in which they have occurred

STRUCTURE
1. Orientation – background information about who, where and when
2. Series of events in chronological order
3. A personal comment (optional)

FEATURES Uses past tense, action verbs, descriptive language, may include quotes

From *Mud, Sweat and Tears*

by Bear Grylls

The air temperature is minus twenty degrees. I wiggle my fingers but they're still freezing cold. Old frostnip injuries never let you forget. I blame Everest for that.
'You set, buddy?' cameraman Simon asks me, smiling. His rig is all prepped and ready.
I smile back. I am unusually nervous.
Something doesn't quite feel right.
But I don't listen to the inner voice.
It is time to go to work.

The crew tell me that the crisp northern Canadian Rockies look spectacular this morning.
I don't really notice.
It is time to get into my secret space. A rare part of me that is focused, clear, brave, precise.
It is the part of me I know the best, but visit the least.
I only like to use it sparingly. Like now.
Beneath me is three hundred feet of steep snow and ice. Steep but manageable.
I have done this sort of fast descent many, many times. Never be complacent, the voice says.
The voice is always right.
A last deep breath. A look to Simon. A silent acknowledgement back.
Yet we have cut a vital corner. I know it. But I do nothing.
I leap.
I am instantly taken by the speed. Normally I love it. This time I am worried.
I never feel worried in the moment.
I know something is wrong.
I am soon travelling at over 40 m.p.h. Feet first down the mountain. The ice races past only inches from my head. This is my world.
I gain even more speed. The edge of the peak gets closer. Time to arrest the fall.
I flip nimbly on to my front and drive the ice axe deep into the mountain with all my power.
It works like it always does. Like clockwork. Total confidence. One of those rare moments of lucidity.
It is fleeting. Then it is gone.
I am now static.
The world hangs still. Then – bang.

Simon, his heavy wooden sledge, plus solid metal camera housing, piles straight into my left thigh. He is doing in excess of 45 m.p.h. There is an instant explosion of pain and noise and white.

It is like a freight train. And I am thrown down the mountain like a doll.
Life stands still. I feel and see it all in slow motion.
Yet in that split second I have only one realisation: a one-degree different course and the sledge's impact would have been with my head. Without doubt, it would have been my last living thought.

  ISBN 9780170260121

On the surface *(Literal comprehension – right-there questions)*

1 Where is this passage set?
2 What is the temperature?
3 How high up are they?
4 How fast was Bear travelling down the hill?
5 How does Simon (the cameraman) descend?
6 What went wrong?

Discovering techniques *(Language structures and features, spelling, grammar, vocabulary)*

1 Find an example of each of the following parts of speech from the sentence below:

a Personal Pronoun
b Noun
c Abstract noun
d Adjective
e Verb
f Adverb
g Preposition.

I flip nimbly on to my front and drive the ice axe deep into the mountain with all my power.

2 Several similes are used in this passage to help create the atmosphere. List three of them.
3 Why are there several very short sentences all beginning with 'I'?

Search and think *(Inferential and interpretive comprehension)*

1 Why doesn't Bear notice the beautiful day and surroundings?
2 What does Bear blame Everest for?
3 Describe the way Bear travels down the mountain and stops.
4 Bear says he was 'unusually nervous'. Copy down several other sentences that show his nervousness.
5 What does the sentence 'This is my world' suggest?

Hidden depths *(Creative comprehension – responding personally, higher-order-thinking skills, making links)*

1 What does this short article tell you about the man, Bear Grylls?
Would it be a good opening for a book about him? Why?
2 Write a creative narrative of a dangerous event you have been involved in. Or base your writing on the action of another person. Try to include a sense of adventure, danger and or tension by using short sentences.

Extend yourself *(Links to real life or other literature, researching, writing, creating, speaking tasks)*

1 Research what Civil Defence recommends goes into a home survival/emergency kit.
2 Watch an episode of *Man vs Wild* and write a review of it encouraging people to watch the programme.
3 Find Bear Grylls' autobiography *Mud, Sweat and Tears* and finish reading it.
Note: there are two versions, one for teenagers and one for adults.

UNIT 20

TEXT TYPE Advertisement

PURPOSE To persuade by putting forward an argument or particular point of view, to sell a product

STRUCTURE (VARIES)
1 Images
2 Written or language (body copy)
3 Sensory appeal – e.g. colour, shape

FEATURES May include images and symbols, facts and figures, logical reasoning, examples, and persuasive or emotive language

LONE STAR

NORTH SHORE
335 - 337 Lake Road, Takapuna ★ ph: 09 488 0291
AUCKLAND
8 Kent Street, Newmarket ★ ph: 09 522 4004
WAITAKERE
3 Totara Ave, New Lynn ★ ph: 09 826 1906
MANUKAU
792 Great South Road, Manukau ★ ph: 09 985 0590
TAURANGA
49 - 51 The Strand ★ ph: 07 571 4111
HAMILTON
185 Victoria Street ★ ph: 07 839 3005
ROTORUA
Cnr Arawa & Amohia Streets ★ ph: 07 349 4040
GISBORNE
Inner Harbour
60 The Esplanade, Shed One ★ ph: 06 868 3257
NEW PLYMOUTH
52 - 58 Gill Street ★ New Plymouth ★ ph: 06 759 0902
NAPIER
Cnr Marine Parade & Emerson Street ★ ph: 06 835 0088
PALMERSTON NORTH
41 - 42 The Square ★ ph: 06 355 1986
WELLINGTON
66 Tory Street ★ ph: 04 385 4848
PETONE
Cnr Jackson & Buick Streets, Wellington ★ ph: 04 568 2555
NELSON
88 - 90 Hardy Street ★ ph: 03 548 1441
CHRISTCHURCH
26 Manchester Street ★ ph: 03 365 7086
PAPANUI
116 Northlands Mall, Christchurch ★ ph: 03 352 6653
RICCARTON
Cnr Riccarton & Waimairi Roads, Christchurch ★ ph: 03 943 9434
WANAKA
50 Cardrona Valley Road ★ ph: 03 443 6901
QUEENSTOWN
14 Brecon Street ★ ph: 03 442 9995
DUNEDIN
417 Princes Street ★ ph: 03 474 1955
INVERCARGILL
Cnr Dee & Leet Streets ★ 03 214 6225

Too Much, Ain't Enough
www.lonestar.co.nz

LONE STAR

MESSAGE TO THE PEOPLE

Thank you for choosing to dine at a Lone Star tonight. For the record our first cafe opened in Manchester Street, Christchurch on September 13th 1988. They were pioneer days in the cafe scene in Christchurch and we like to think of ourselves as trailblazers.

Ours was a simple concept, to make dining out fun and to have plenty of it ourselves. To offer generous servings of lovingly prepared and cooked comfort food (similar to what all of our wonderful Kiwi mums cooked) that was fantastic value for money. Strangely enough you took the concept to your hearts and because of you we prospered.

Like all businesses there were plenty of harsh lessons to be learned but we've always remained true to those original values. In 1991 the famous Lone Star Queenstown opened and this legendary cafe showcased our brand to the people of New Zealand and the world. The rest as they say is history. There are now over twenty Lone Stars around New Zealand and we now play a big part in this countries dining out scene, serving nearly a million meals to New Zealanders every year and employing thousands of young Kiwis in the process.

We are very proud of that fact and that we are still 100% New Zealand owned and operated.

Its been the most wonderful ride and we thank you all for being such loyal Lone Star fans over the past twenty years. Finally, our dream for the future is that your children's children will still be coming to the cafe for a special night of Lone Star fun and food in 50 years time.

Amen to that.

Be Staunch, Walk Tall

LONE STAR
NEW ZEALAND

Steinlager CLASSIC

CHRISTCHURCH ★ QUEENSTOWN ★ DUNEDIN ★ INVERCARGILL ★ HAMILTON ★ AUCKLAND ★ WELLINGTON ★ PALMERSTON NORTH ★ NORTH SHORE ★ NELSON ★ WAITAKERE ★ MANUKAU ★ NEW PLYMOUTH ★ PAPANUI ★ RICCARTON ★ PETONE ★ GISBORNE
www.lonestar.co.nz

ISBN 9780170260121

On the surface *(Literal comprehension – right-there questions)*

1 How long has Lone Star been operating?
2 Where was a Lone Star opened in 1991?
3 How many cities and towns have a Lone Star?
4 What are the owners of Lone Star very proud of?
5 What type of Kiwis does a Lone Star employ?

Discovering techniques *(Language structures and features, spelling, grammar, vocabulary)*

1 List the words that connect to 'cowboys on the frontier'.
2 Find examples of personal pronouns in this pamphlet and explain why they would have been used.
3 There are two grammatical mistakes in the central column of text. Can you find them?

Search and think *(Inferential and interpretive comprehension)*

1 What is 'simple' about the Lone Star concept?
2 Look at the three taglines (advertising catchphrases) below. Explain the message in each of these and how each relates to the rest of the information in the phamplet.
   - Too Much, Ain't Enough
   - Amen to that.
   - Be Staunch, Walk Tall
3 Where do they suggest you go for a 'daily meal deal'?
4 Explain the link between the images (pictures) and the text (words). Think 'Wild West'. Use examples from the text to support your answer.
5 The cowboy concept is very American. What words/phrases in the central column show that Lone Star is a New Zealand business?

Hidden depths *(Creative comprehension – responding personally, higher-order-thinking skills, making links)*

1 This material is also found on the Lone Star menu. Why would they put this type of information on it?
2 The restaurant is named Lone Star. Who was the 'Lone Star' of the American Wild West?

Extend yourself *(Links to real life or other literature, researching, writing, creating, speaking tasks)*

1 Go online and search for the actual Lone Star menu. Make connections between the theme and the names of the meals they serve.
2 Imagine you owned a Lone Star and have been asked as the owner to provide a new recipe for the menu. Describe the meal you would design.
3 Find two examples of similar 'themed' restaurant advertisements/placements. Compare the content by looking for similarities and differences. Which do you prefer and why?

UNIT 21

TEXT TYPE Description
PURPOSE To describe the characteristic features of a particular thing
STRUCTURE 1 Opening statement – introduction to the subject
2 Characteristic features of the subject
3 Concluding comment (optional)
FEATURES Details involving senses to assist readers to visualise a scene or event.

From *The Keeper* by Barry Faville

THE VOLCANO'S ROAR WAS UNDIMINISHED, IN FACT IT SEEMED TO BE REACHING A CRESCENDO. Even several kilometres away we could feel the heat on our cheeks. Then there was an even mightier explosion, an echoing boom, as the lava column leapt higher than before. The ground shook and then writhed in a quake that sent us sprawling. I remember seeing earth moving in waves and ripples, like a mat being flicked in the wind to clean out dust. The domed roof of the arms dump swelled and collapsed inwards with a dull thud. I saw a couple of shadowy figures totter from the doorway before it disappeared in a billow of dust. From inside there was silence.

At precisely this instant I heard the sound that still sends shivers up my back when I recall it – a dry, crackling noise accompanied by a soft, endless hiss. I turned. A bright orange river was spilling over the volcano's cone and flowing down the slope in broad torrents. Red hot lava was pouring towards us. Two images stick forever in my mind: the lava flowing like water, yet seeming to restrain itself, as though its steep plunge should not be over too quickly; then the tongues of lava sliding up and down over every hollow and gully, their tips glowing orange, covered with black scabs where the molten material had partly cooled, seeming to lick at every scrap of vegetation in their path. Burning tussock and incinerated earth gave off the sounds I had heard. As the tongue tips approached, the ground scorched and burned, hissing and crackling and dying.

The bulging, orange tongues poised for a few seconds on the edge of the valley above us, then began to slither downwards in a rush. We ran. I ran blindly. I had only one thought in my mind: to reach the opposite side of the valley and the rising slopes before my feet and ankles were grabbed and held by that awful, burning orange. Steam and smoke swirled around my head, the sky roared and hissed, and I could not suck enough air into my lungs because it seemed to have melted into fire that was trying to engulf me. I could not tell whether the endless roar was inside or outside my head.

ISBN 9780170260121

On the surface *(Literal comprehension – right-there questions)*

1 How far away could they feel the heat of the volcano?
2 What sent them sprawling?
3 What type of building collapsed after the earthquake?
4 The author compared the partly cooled lava to what?
5 Where was he trying to run/escape to?

Discovering techniques *(Language structures and features, spelling, grammar, vocabulary)*

1 Find at least one example of each of the following language techniques.
   a Alliteration
   b Onomatopoeia
   c Metaphor
   d Personification
   e Simile
2 A metaphor that is repeated through a passage is referred to as an 'extended metaphor'. Find examples of an extended metaphor in this extract.

Search and think *(Inferential and interpretive comprehension)*

1 What do you think happened at the arms dump? Explain your answer.
2 Why did he 'run blindly'?
3 He says: 'I could not tell whether the endless roar was inside or outside my head.' What does he mean?
4 This extract concentrates on the character's experience of these natural events. Summarise how the writer does this.

Hidden depths *(Creative comprehension – responding personally, higher-order-thinking skills, making links)*

1 How effective is the passage in capturing your attention? Do you want to keep on reading? What do you want to know?

Extend yourself *(Links to real life or other literature, researching, writing, creating, speaking tasks)*

1 Pick another type of natural disaster and write a descriptive passage.
2 Research two volcanic eruptions in New Zealand.
3 Research two earthquakes in New Zealand.

ISBN 9780170260121

UNIT 22

TEXT TYPE Advertisement

PURPOSE To persuade by putting forward an argument or particular point of view, to sell a product

STRUCTURE (VARIES)
1. Images
2. Written or spoken language
3. Sensory appeal – e.g. colour, shape

FEATURES May include images, facts and figures, logical reasoning, examples, and persuasive or emotive language

ISBN 9780170260121

On the surface *(Literal comprehension – right-there questions)*

1. What BurgerFuel product is this advertising?
2. How much extra will you pay for a gluten free bun?
3. The gluten free bun is being promoted as a healthy alternative to what?
4. The gluten free bun is also free of which other ingredients?
5. Who helped BurgerFuel trial their product?

Discovering techniques *(Language structures and features, spelling, grammar, vocabulary)*

1. List the personal pronouns used in this advertisement and how often each is used. Explain why you think there are so many of them.
2. Copy down the BurgerFuel slogan.
3. Why is the BurgerFuel logo found on both sides of the advertisement?
4. Why are some words in bold and centred?
5. There is an allusion to a movie and a metaphor linked to the pictures in the text. Find them.

Search and think *(Inferential and interpretive comprehension)*

1. Find as many links between the verbal elements and the visual elements of this advertisement as you can.
2. Who is the target audience for this advertisement?
3. List the other BurgerFuel products promoted in this advertisement.
4. Read the words aloud. What do you notice about the tone?
5. Why might someone who is severely intolerant still need to avoid products at BurgerFuel?
6. Why would an advertisement such as this put the following sentence on their advertisement?

   'Information was correct at the time of print.'

Hidden depths *(Creative comprehension – responding personally, higher-order-thinking skills, making links)*

1. Do you consider this to be a successful advertisement? Why or why not?
2. Create an advertisement for a product that appeals to the health conscious person. Perhaps an allergy-related product (gluten, dairy, egg, nut, etc).
3. What is gluten? Write a paragraph following the structure you use in your class for a formal essay.
4. BurgerFuel has some creative titles for their products. I.e Motobites, Hamburgini, Third Pounder etc. Have some fun creating some titles and descriptors for a fast food or cake shop menu. You might link this to a theme e.g. sport, vehicles, colours, characters etc.

Extend yourself *(Links to real life or other literature, researching, writing, creating, speaking tasks)*

1. Research what it is about gluten that makes it something that many people are now avoiding.
2. Research how other fast food chains are trying to have better options for people with allergies.
3. Survey your classmates. How many people have (or know people who have) food allergies? The answer may surprise you. Present your results visually.
4. Is BurgerFuel a New Zealand company? How long has it existed? Where else does it sell its products? Does it compete with the major fast food outlets? Find out all you can about the company.

ISBN 9780170260121

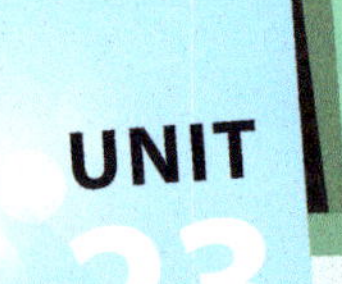

UNIT 23

TEXT TYPE Advertorial
PURPOSE To inform and persuade
STRUCTURE Orientation – background information
Series of statements in logical progression
FEATURES Facts and figures, formal language, positive vocabulary

"FOR 30 YEARS WE'VE PUT OUR CUSTOMERS, OUR PEOPLE, OUR COMMUNITIES AND THE ENVIRONMENT AT THE CORE OF WHAT WE DO – IT'S PART OF OUR DNA."

Mark Powell, The Warehouse Group CEO

The original Warehouse store in 1982

bargaining ON MAKING A DIFFERENCE

If you mention The Big Red Shed in New Zealand, a large percentage of the population would know the establishment you are talking about.

The Warehouse is part of the common Kiwi vernacular, and its tagline 'where everyone gets a bargain' is a well sung jingle by many a pre-schooler. There's no denying that in the past 30 years it has become a favourite store for many Kiwis.

In fact, The Warehouse now has a full online offer and 92 stores nationwide, carrying a wide range of products from clothing, entertainment, technology and music to sporting, gardening, grocery and many others. Around 95% of the country's population lives within a 30-minute drive of a Warehouse store, scattered in 58 towns and cities. It claims unrivalled coverage in New Zealand non-food retailing.

Founded in 1982 by Stephen (now Sir Stephen) and Margaret Tindall with a very small store on Auckland's North Shore, it was first listed on the New Zealand Stock Exchange in 1994.

Today The Warehouse is more than a store; it's an establishment that does a lot of the community. In the past 30 years the company has raised over $20 million to support Kiwi community organisations and its commitment is such that Community and Environment is one of the key focuses of its overall business.

However, also at the forefront of its business is its commitment to sustainability. This can be seen in many ways: in its commitment to reducing the number of bags issued at the checkouts through to monitoring sources and suppliers from offshore through its 'ethical sourcing efforts'. The company is committed to communities that contribute to the supply chain of The Warehouse in countries where products are manufactured, and this is reflected in the company's Ethical Sourcing policy.

The Warehouse is the only major New Zealand retailer to account for its performance with respect to community and the environment through its annual Community and Environment Report.

'At The Warehouse, we recognise that choices we make today affect the future environment. We need to play our part in ensuring that growth today does not compromise opportunities for future generations. To be a sustainable business we need to extend our conscience beyond immediate commercial objectives. Scientific knowledge about the scarcity of natural resources and man's impact on the environment impels us to take greater responsibility for the environmental characteristics of our operations and the products we sell.' (Extracted from *The Warehouse Sustainability Charter 2009*)

The Warehouse has implemented a Community and Environment management forum, which has developed and implemented new strategies and initiatives such as the 'Great TV Takeback' event, where customers could return their old televisions – 28,000 were returned.

Another step in its measures to reduce its carbon footprint is partnering with Toyota New Zealand to replace all its passenger fleet cars with hybrid vehicles.

The purchase of the 34 hybrid cars will have a great impact on The Warehouse's energy consumption and CO_2 emissions, cutting its CO_2 emissions by up to 40%. The other benefits of the hybrid car switch include lower fuel use, lower greenhouse gas emissions and less exhaust air pollution.

  ISBN 9780170260121

On the surface *(Literal comprehension – right-there questions)*

1 What is the other name used for The Warehouse?
2 Two names are given for the phrase 'where everyone gets a bargain'. What are they?
3 How many stores does The Warehouse have nationwide?
4 When and where was The Warehouse founded?
5 In the past 30 years, what has the company raised over $20 million to support?
6 The Warehouse is committed to two key focuses. What are they?

Discovering techniques *(Language structures and features, spelling, grammar, vocabulary)*

1 Why is the word 'Kiwi' written with a capital letter when it is used in this passage?
2 Which phrase suggests that The Warehouse is popular in New Zealand?
3 What does the phrase 'unrivalled coverage' mean?
4 Inverted commas surround four sentences in the article. Why?

Search and think *(Inferential and interpretive comprehension)*

1 What does the line 'well sung jingle by many a pre-schooler' suggest?
2 How many times is the word 'community' used in this article? Why is it used so often?
3 How does buying hybrid cars link to one of The Warehouse's key focuses?

Hidden depths *(Creative comprehension – responding personally, higher-order-thinking skills, making links)*

1 We have identified this passage as 'advertorial'. What is an advertorial? How does this piece fit that definition?
2 The article makes much of the widespread reach of The Warehouse. Is there a downside to this nationwide presence? What about the effect of The Warehouse in your home town?

Extend yourself *(Links to real life or other literature, researching, writing, creating, speaking tasks)*

1 The Warehouse is praised for reducing the number of plastic bags used by its customers. Why is this important in the world today?
2 Research two other significant events that occurred in New Zealand during 1982.
3 Research another New Zealand company that has a similar commitment to 'sustainability'. What do they do?

ISBN 9780170260121

UNIT 24

TEXT TYPE Explanation

PURPOSE To inform, to explain how or why things are as they are, or how things work

STRUCTURE
1 A general statement
2 Series of statement or events in chronological or logical order
3 Concluding statement

FEATURES Logical sequence of details or ideas may use heading, diagrams and tables

ENROL AND VOTE FOR THE FIRST TIME

Every year, thousands of New Zealanders become eligible to enrol to vote for the first time, and this section of the website will help you get on the roll and ready to vote.

New Zealanders are lucky to live in a democracy, and we can all play our part in keeping our democracy strong by getting on the electoral roll and voting. It means we can take part in local elections, when we choose the people who will make decisions about our local areas, and general elections, when we choose the parties and politicians who will represent us in Parliament.

It also means we get to have a say on big national issues through public referenda.

Who can enrol?

In New Zealand the law says that you must be enrolled on the electoral roll. You must enrol if you:

- are 18 years or older, and
- have lived in New Zealand for more than one year continuously at some time in your life, and
- are a New Zealand citizen, or
- are a permanent resident of New Zealand*.

* Cook Island Maori, Niueans and Tokelauans can enrol once they have lived in New Zealand continuously for 12 months. They do not require permanent residency to be eligible to enrol and vote.

Only those who are enrolled can vote, take part in a referendum, or sign a petition.

You can provisionally enrol when you are 17 by filling in an enrolment form. You will then be automatically enrolled on your 18th birthday.

There are only a few reasons why a person cannot enrol. Find out who is excluded from enrolling.

How do I enrol?

Getting on the roll is easy! You can get on the roll now, or get a form sent to you by Free texting your name and address to 3676 or calling 0800 36 76 56. You can also pick up a form at your local PostShop. The form will ask you for information about yourself. Find out what the form will ask and why.

When you have enrolled, your name will go on the electoral roll, which is the list of people who have enrolled and are allowed to vote.

If you are Māori, you get to choose whether you want to be on the Māori or the General Roll. Find out more about the choice to go on the Maori or the General Roll.

If you are concerned about your safety if your name goes on the Electoral Roll, you can ask to go on the Unpublished Roll. Find out more about the Unpublished Roll.

If you need help to fill in your form, because of language or disability issues, you can ask someone else to help you, or you can contact your local Registrar of Electors.

How do I vote?

Every three years New Zealand holds a general election. This is when you choose the people and political parties who will make the decisions about the way New Zealand is run.

In New Zealand, we use a voting system called MMP. In a general election, you have two votes. The first vote is the party vote, where you vote for the political party that you most want to see in Parliament. A political party with a lot of votes will have more Members of Parliament. The political party or parties with the most votes become the Government.

With your second vote you can choose the person you most want to be your local Member of Parliament. They will represent your electorate, which is the geographical region you are enrolled in. The person who gets the most votes in your electorate will be your local Member of Parliament.

Find out more about how our MMP voting system works.

On the surface *(Literal comprehension – right-there questions)*

1 How old do you have to be to provisionally enrol?
2 Is it law to be enrolled on the electoral roll?
3 How many types of elections are there for you to take part in if you are on the electoral roll?
4 How long do Cook Island Maori, Niueans and Tokelauans have to have lived in New Zealand continuously for before they can enrol?
5 How many ways are there for you to get an enrolment form? List them.

Discovering techniques *(Language structures and features, spelling, grammar, vocabulary)*

1 What does the acronym MMP stand for?
2 Why is an asterisk (*) used?
3 Comment on the use of pronouns in the section How Do I Vote?
4 Look up the word 'parliament'. Where does it come from?
5 Considering this text has been taken from a webpage, what do you think the words in orange are?

Search and think *(Inferential and interpretive comprehension)*

1 Our system of government is called a 'democracy'. What does this word mean? Where does it originate?
2 Why is it important to vote for your area's Member of Parliament?
3 Go to the website (www.elections.org.nz) and read the rest of this page. What possible worries might people have about voting?
4 What is the electoral roll?

Hidden depths *(Creative comprehension – responding personally, higher-order-thinking skills, making links)*

1 What is a 'referendum'? Name three issues New Zealanders have been asked to vote on by referendum.
2 What additional decisions are there for some potential voters?

Extend yourself *(Links to real life or other literature, researching, writing, creating, speaking tasks)*

1 The information states that we are lucky to live in a democracy. We get to vote for Parliament once every three years. But is there more to democracy than just elections? What else is important, do you think? What do people in other countries that are not democracies want for themselves?
2 Find out which other countries use the MMP voting system.
3 What is the Maori Roll?
4 Who is your Member of Parliament? Do you think they are working well for your community?

ISBN 9780170260121

UNIT 25

TEXT TYPE Recount

PURPOSE To reconstruct past experiences by retelling events in the order in which they have occurred

STRUCTURE
1 Orientation – background information about who, where and when
2 Series of events in chronological order
3 A personal comment (optional)

FEATURES Uses past tense, action verbs, descriptive language, may include quotes

KARETU SCHOOL MURAL PROJECT

HOW IT CAME ABOUT ...

In Term 4 2010, the Year 7s and 8s of Karetu School went to Australia for their biennial Sydney trip. Teacher Cherie Anderson wanted a project equally as exciting for her remaining Year 6s, so they decided to use the time to create a backdrop for the school play. Ms Anderson recruited the help of her sister – artist Simone Anderson – who packed up her family, travelled North (from Tauranga) and 'moved in' for the week to help with the project. The seniors worked with Simone discussing inspirations and values, and tried to capture this all on the mural. As well as inspiration coming from the environment and Maoritanga, they were influenced by Friedensreich Hundertwasser, who had lived in this community. Every child in the school participated in the props for the school play in some way. The younger children were busy making leaves and lollipop trees and flowers while the older children worked away at the background.

Karetu School is a picturesque three teacher, Decile 3 country school situated on the beautiful Karetu valley, 10 kilometres away from Kawakawa. We are a school that prides itself on delivering small class sizes within a safe family-orientated environment. The focus of everything we do is firmly upon the children and their present and future well-being.

'There is no denying that we ended up creating something well beyond our dreams or expectations. We quickly realised that it was too special to fold up and lose in a cupboard after the play, and now thanks to Keep New Zealand Beautiful, we are able to reconstruct it in a permanent form for the whole community to enjoy.'

THE PROJECT

In November 2011, the children of Karetu School downed pens, picked up paint brushes, dusted off their creativity and reconstructed their fabulous backdrop in a more permanent form on the 12 m by 2.9 m wall in Kawakawa.

Again, working with artist Simone Anderson, they transformed the wall into an icon the town will be proud of. Over the week groups of children worked on site preparing the wall, while others worked back at school. The dedication was amazing, with parents and kids staying until the evenings to ensure the project was completed within the time frame. Copper, stainless steel, handmade ceramic shapes, plywood cut-out shapes and mosaics using recycled aluminium cans were all used to create a three dimensional factor.

Recycled materials were used in keeping with our Enviroschools teachings and the philosophies of Hundertwasser himself.

As with the original mural, every child in the school participated in some way, painting backgrounds, making leaves or Hundertwasser-style lollipop trees. If you look closely you will notice that part of the sky is created with handprints. Every hand that worked on the mural was captured!

  ISBN 9780170260121

On the surface *(Literal comprehension – right-there questions)*

1 Which school created the mural?
2 Where is the school located?
3 What was the artwork originally created for?
4 Who did Ms Anderson get to help the students create the backdrop?
5 How large is the permanent mural?

Discovering techniques *(Language structures and features, spelling, grammar, vocabulary)*

1 Why does the writer use a metaphor to say Simone 'packed up' her family?
2 There is an example of direct quotation in the report. Write down the first and last words. Whose words are they?
3 Why do the words 'Keep New Zealand Beautiful' all have capital letters?
4 Which adjective is used to describe the backdrop?
5 In the box at the end of the report the writer uses a personal pronoun. Which one and why?

Search and think *(Inferential and interpretive comprehension)*

1 How is every student represented in the mural?
2 The school advertises that:

    We are a school that prides itself on delivering small class sizes within a safe family-orientated environment.

    How is this reflected in construction of the mural?
3 What were the three philosophies that they kept in mind while creating the mural?

Hidden depths *(Creative comprehension – responding personally, higher-order-thinking skills, making links)*

1 What were Hundertwasser's philosophies?
2 What else did Hundertwasser contribute to the 'facilities' in Kawakawa?
3 What is Keep New Zealand Beautiful? What does it do?
4 Design a mural in the same Hundertwasser style that represents your school or community.

Extend yourself *(Links to real life or other literature, researching, writing, creating, speaking tasks)*

1 Research Friedensreich Hundertwasser. Why is he famous internationally? Why did he live in New Zealand?
2 Find some examples of his work and explain in writing, speech or images your personal response to his work.
3 Investigate the way Maoritanga and environmental concerns are linked. Present your findings in words or images.

ISBN 9780170260121

UNIT 26

TEXT TYPE Poem
PURPOSE To express ideas in precise and powerful language
STRUCTURE Lines, rhyme, rhythm, verses
FEATURES Careful word choice for meaning and sound, figurative language, verse, rhyme, imagery

BEHIND the SCENES

The actor struts his little hour,
Between the limelight and the band;
The public feel the actor's power,
Yet nothing do they understand

Of all the touches here and there
That make or mar the actor's part,
They never see, beneath the glare,
The artist striving after art.

To them it seems a labour slight
Where nought of study intervenes;
You see it in another light
When once you've been behind the scenes.

For though the actor at his best
Is, like a poet, born not made,
He still must study with a zest
And practise hard to learn his trade.

So, whether on the actor's form
The stately robes of Hamlet sit,
Or as Macbeth he rave and storm,
Or plays burlesque to please the pit,

'Tis each and all a work of art,
That constant care and practice means–
The actor who creates a part
Has done his work behind the scenes.

By Banjo Patterson

On the surface *(Literal comprehension – right-there questions)*

1 The poem is about a job. Which job?
2 What does the public think about the difficulty of this work?
3 What other sort of work is this work compared with?
4 Which lines tell you the writer understands this work is hard work?
5 Which two acting roles are named?

Discovering techniques *(Language structures and features, spelling, grammar, vocabulary)*

1 What is the verse structure of the poem?
2 Find an example of alliteration.
3 Use a dictionary to find the meanings of the following words as they are used in the text. Note more than one meaning for each linked to the poem's topic.
   a Burlesque
   b Pit
   c Limelight
4 Find an example of repetition in the poem.

Search and think *(Inferential and interpretive comprehension)*

1 Using your understanding of the words 'pit' and 'limelight' explain the meaning of line 2.
2 Explain what you understand by the line 'You see it in another light'.
3 What varieties of performance does the poet mention?
4 This poem was published in 1893. Is its message old-fashioned? Explain your answer.

Hidden depths *(Creative comprehension – responding personally, higher-order-thinking skills, making links)*

1 The poet compares the work of an actor to that of a poet. Why?
2 Comment on the double meaning of the title of the poem.

Extend yourself *(Links to real life or other literature, researching, writing, creating, speaking tasks)*

1 Find out more about Banjo Patterson, the poet.
2 Choose one of Patterson's narrative poems and copy it. Learn at least the first verse by heart.
3 Try writing a short poem with an equal number of syllables in each line and a regular rhyme pattern yourself. See how hard it is!
4 Explain how 'practice makes perfect' applies to something you do.

ISBN 9780170260121

UNIT
27

TEXT TYPE Explanation
PURPOSE To inform, to explain how or why things are as they are, or how things work
STRUCTURE
1 A general statement
2 Series of statement or events in chronological or logical order
3 Concluding statement
FEATURES Logical sequence of details or ideas may use heading, diagrams and tables

Powhiri

The powhiri is the ritual ceremony of encounter. Traditionally the process served to discover whether the visiting party were friend or foe, and so its origins lay partly in military necessity. As the ceremony progressed, and after friendly intent was established, it became a formal welcoming of guests (manuhiri) by the hosts (tangata whenua or home people). As the ceremony progresses also, the tapu or sacredness surrounding manuhiri is removed, and they become one with the tangata whenua.

It begins with the **karanga**, the high-pitched voices of women from both sides, calling to each other to exchange information to begin to establish intent and the purpose of the visit. It is said that the kaikaranga (callers) between them weave a mat laid upon Papatuanuku (Mother Earth) binding the two sides together, and protecting Her from the men who will verbally, and perhaps physically, joust with each other.

In traditional times a **wero** or challenge was performed by a warrior or warriors, advancing on the manuhiri to look them over and further establish intent. The wero is sometimes performed today, particularly for the most prestigious manuhiri.

The tangata whenua will perform the **haka powhiri**, a chant and dance of welcome, during which the manuhiri are symbolically drawn onto the marae (sacred courtyard). The chants often use the symbolism of hauling a waka or canoe onto the shore.

Next is the **mihi** or exchange of greetings by the orators (usually male) from both sides. Oratory is much prized. An expert will display his knowledge of whakapapa (genealogy and history) and mythology, and his mastery of language, rhetoric and dramatic presentation. During whaikorero (speechmaking) links between the ancestors and the living are made, and genealogical links between tangata whenua and manuhiri are emphasised. The kaupapa or purpose of the occasion will be discussed, and perhaps general present day issues and concerns might be aired.

Each speech is followed by the performance of a **waiata** (song), or sometimes a haka (dance), by the orator's support group. The quality of the performance is a matter of critical concern, and reflects on the orator, and the orator's party.

At the completion of their speeches the manuhiri will present a **koha** to the tangata whenua. Today it is usually in the form of money, but in the past it would have been food or valued possessions.

Then the manuhiri move across the marae to **hongi** with the tangata whenua. The hongi is a gentle pressing of noses, and signifies the mingling together of the sacred breath of life, and the two sides become one.

The powhiri concludes with the sharing of kai or food, called **hakari**. The food removes the tapu or sacredness from the manuhiri, so that the two sides may complete the coming together. As in all cultures the sharing of food also signifies a binding together.

  ISBN 9780170260121

On the surface *(Literal comprehension – right-there questions)*

1 What is a powhiri?
2 What do the women on both sides do at the start of the powhiri?
3 Who gives the mihi?
4 What does the word 'waiata' mean?
5 What does the powhiri conclude with?
6 How many parts are there to a powhiri? List them.

Discovering techniques *(Language structures and features, spelling, grammar, vocabulary)*

1 Why is the second paragraph written mostly in the past tense?
2 Why is the rest of the passage written in the present tense?
3 How does the structure of the passage (i.e. order of the paragraphs) reflect the powhiri's structure?
4 Most of the brackets used have one purpose. What purpose?

Search and think *(Inferential and interpretive comprehension)*

1 Why would it be important to establish friendly intent early on in a powhiri?
2 What is the significance of the symbol of the mat in paragraph two?
3 Many Maori words have made their way into New Zealand English. This article is full of such examples. Write two lists: one of Maori words you already knew the meaning of and the other of Maori words that you have learnt the meaning of from this passage.
4 Which part of the powhiri does the writer say is the most important? Why?

Hidden depths *(Creative comprehension – responding personally, higher-order-thinking skills, making links)*

1 Why do you think the haka powhiri often have actions that symbolise the hauling of a waka or canoe onto the shore?
2 The passage mentions how mythology may be woven into the powhiri. Research one Maori myth that is used in powhiri. Write the story of the myth.
3 Oratory is the word used to describe the art of public speaking. It refers to the eloquence or skill in making speeches to the public. This article says that 'oratory is much prized'. Why do you think this would be so?

Extend yourself *(Links to real life or other literature, researching, writing, creating, speaking tasks)*

1 The word 'tapu' is used to describe the sanctity of the visitors. It also carries the idea of 'forbidden'. It is a very important concept for Maori. Research its original meaning. How is this word used in our New Zealand world today?
2 Research a ritual or ceremony from another culture (perhaps your own) and write a similar article.

   You might look at another welcoming ceremony or you may choose to look at something else: a wedding ceremony, a funeral, a christening or baptism, a baby shower, a bar mitzvah, a 21st birthday, a graduation. Think about rituals in your own culture.

   Remember to follow the structure outlined at the top of this unit.

UNIT 28

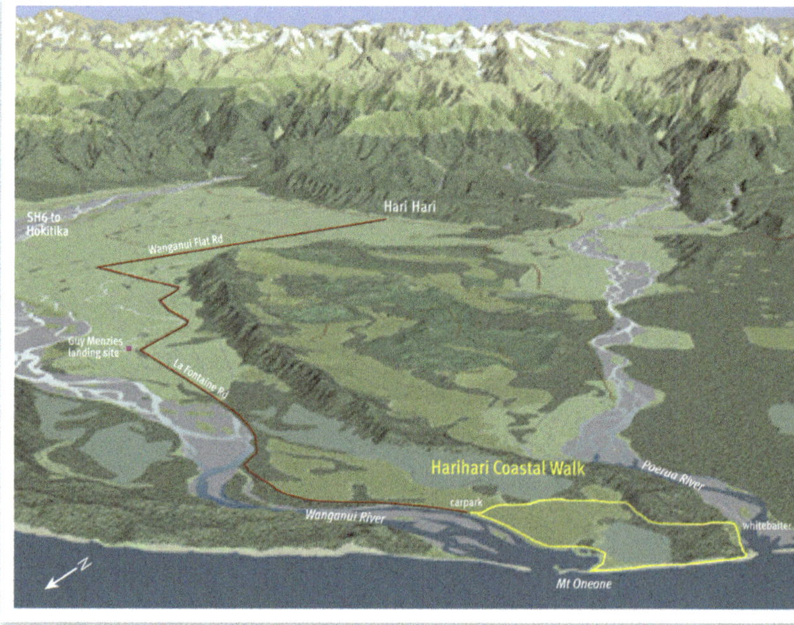

TEXT TYPE Explanation (of walking route)
PURPOSE To provide information, to encourage participation
STRUCTURE Logical sequence of information
FEATURES Instructions, persuasive language

HARIHARI
COASTAL WALK

State Highway 6, which traverses much of the length of the West Coast, is one of the country's most scenic drives. Many motorists find it somewhat surprising, then, that so few sections follow the actual coastline. This walk provides a not-to-be-missed opportunity to experience coastal Westland.

Accessible from the town of Harihari, the well-benched track loops between the Wanganui and Poerua river mouths, traversing luxuriant coastal forests past whitebaiters' baches, and crossing pakihi wetlands to a section of coast where the forest rubs shoulders with the sea.

The coastal section can be safely walked only within 2-3 hours either side of low tide; DOC posts tide tables at the carpark, or they are available in the local newspaper, the *West Coast Times*.

This is an ideal family walk, with mainly flat, easy walking. It is worth attempting even when rain seems likely: the coast receives far less precipitation than inland areas where during westerly weather the mountains enforce heavy orographic rainfall.

Road to Mt Oneone and Poerua River Mouth
60-75 minutes

From the carpark the track heads towards the sea, passing a junction (where the loop ends) after 2 minutes. Keep right. Boardwalked sections avoid most of the potentially muddy track. During spring this part of the track is used mostly by whitebaiters accessing their stands on the Wanganui River.

After 30-40 minutes the track emerges onto the estuarine mouth of the Wanganui River, where Mt Oneone (56m) forms a prominent wedge on the skyline. The hill formed after retreating glaciers deposited moraine some 16,000-18,000 years ago. Follow yellow and blue poles around the estuary shore amongst piles of logs and debris (washed up from the river's frequent spates) to reach the base of Mt Oneone. Unfortunately the unstable nature of the hilltop has forced DOC to close the side-track which leads out to the coast after another few minutes.

Head south along the shore, on pebble-strewn sands at first, then amongst boulders cast down from the cliffs near the Poerua River mouth. Watch out for the yellow and blue posts where the track heads inland.

Poerua River Mouth and Carpark
1.5 hours

After cresting a small rise, the track descends to near the Poerua River, where some whitebaiters' baches are located. In times past, Maori had summer eeling camps situated here. From the coast, the track cuts across a low rise – another moraine deposit now heavily forested. There's a seat with a view over the pakihi wetland. The track descends to cross an arm of this wetland, and then the Oneone River on a footbridge. Kahikatea, New Zealand's tallest tree, dominates the area, and during the 1930s an industry sprang up to mill the wood, which proved ideal for butter boxes. The last section of track follows a straight section of the old logging tramway used to haul out logs to nearby timber mills. Operations ceased in the late 1950s. The loop concludes 2 minutes before the carpark.

Grade	Easy
Maps	134 Harihari
Total Walking Time	2.5-3 hours

Access
The walk starts from a carpark on La Fontaine Road, 20 km from Harihari (with the last 8 km gravel). The turnoff from SH 6 (onto Wanganui Flat Road) is signposted, along with the turn onto La Fontaine Road. En route, walkers may like to visit the historic site where Australian pioneer aviator Guy Menzies crash-landed in a swamp after completing the first solo trans Tasman flight in 1931.

Alternative route
The Wanganui River mouth makes a worthwhile trip for those who have less time or meet unfavourable tides (60-80 minutes return).

Information
DOC Franz Josef Tel: 03-752-0796

ISBN 9780170260121

On the surface *(Literal comprehension – right-there questions)*

1 What is the closest settlement to this walk?
2 When can the part of the walk along the coast be walked safely?
3 When did Mt Oneone form?
4 What helps keep walkers on the track?
5 On the graphic, which places does SH6 connect?
6 What is New Zealand's tallest tree?

Discovering techniques *(Language structures and features, spelling, grammar, vocabulary)*

1 Use a dictionary to find the meanings of the following words as they are used in the text:
   a luxuriant
   b moraine
   c estuarine
   d spates
   e orographic
2 There is an example of personification in the first section. What is it? What is its effect?
3 Find two examples of imperatives (commands).
4 What is the purpose of the arrow on the graphic?

Search and think *(Inferential and interpretive comprehension)*

1 There are five sections to this article. What is the difference between them?
2 What is DOC? What work does DOC do on the Harihari Coastal Walk? Why?

Hidden depths *(Creative comprehension – responding personally, higher-order-thinking skills, making links)*

1 How does the writing encourage people to take this walk?
2 The writing suggests interesting features that potential visitors might enjoy. List as many as you can. Can you group them?

Extend yourself *(Links to real life or other literature, researching, writing, creating, speaking tasks)*

1 Choose an area you know well and create a similar guide for a short walk. Include some encouragement, some direct instructions about the route, a map, interesting local facts and a quick reference box.
2 Research whitebaiting on the West Coast of New Zealand.
3 Find out about Guy Menzies.

UNIT 29

TEXT TYPE From the Editor

PURPOSE to introduce an edition of the magazine

STRUCTURE
1. Salutation to readers
2. Mention selection of content
3. Link in to magazine

FEATURES conversational tone, persuasive language, positive words, personal pronouns, direct address to reader

makeover magic

From the movies to real life, Sarah talks transitions.

You know that feeling when you're genuinely so super-excited about something that you just can't sit still? Well, that's how I felt about putting Demi Lovato on the cover of *Girlfriend*. So much so that I did a victory lap of the office to celebrate once the ink had dried. You see, Demi is not only an amazing singer – she is also a fantastic role model for teens. And her new single "Heart Attack" has been playing on repeat on Spotify in the *Girlfriend* office since its release. I've been watching Demi for a while now and the transformation she has made from Disney princess to pop star. I don't know about you, but I'm a sucker for a makeover. In movies they're hands down my favourite scenes, and now it's time for me to give myself one. By the time you read this, I will be winging my way to the UK where the European me will become the new me. European me won't trip over my own feet, suffer from foot-in-mouth or need chocolate to survive. And although I know moving countries won't make me any less clumsy, I'm super-excited for the adventure. So with a heavy heart, it's now my turn to say goodbye. I have been at *Girlfriend* for a good time, not a long time, but I have loved every minute of it. Whether we met through the pages of the magazine, online through social media or at the 2013 Girlfriend Model Search, I have thoroughly enjoyed getting to know you – our readers. Like they say, as one door closes another one opens, and this new door is very exciting for you *GF* readers. There's a new lady in the driver's seat, and she's a pretty cool chick. Rebecca drives around blasting 1D, but she also hearts Lana del Ray. And like us, she totally loves J.Law and can't wait for the second Hunger Games film. So your fave mag is in excellent hands. Thanks for the ride, girls – it's been a blast. See ya!

Sarah x

The sky's the limit, so aim high and embrace change.

On the surface *(Literal comprehension – right-there questions)*

1 Who and what is the 'I' writing this passage? Who is the 'you'?
2 What faults does Sarah admit to?
3 Where has Sarah gone?
4 Who is the new Editor?
5 What web-based media are mentioned on the page?

Discovering techniques *(Language structures and features, spelling, grammar, vocabulary)*

1 What figure of speech opens this passage?
2 There are several examples of alliteration. List as many as you can find.
3 Find one example of a metaphor and explain its meaning.
4 Find three examples of colloquial language.

Search and think *(Inferential and interpretive comprehension)*

1 The writer uses several clichés. Give at least two examples and explain why she uses clichés.
2 Why are no surnames used?
3 Choose one of the pictures accompanying the article and explain how it and the graphical elements on the picture link to the text.
4 Comment on how the layout of the text makes it easy to read.
5 Why is the title of this passage 'Makeover Magic'?

Hidden depths *(Creative comprehension – responding personally, higher-order-thinking skills, making links)*

1 This is written for a girls' magazine. Write a similar piece for a boys' magazine. If you are a girl ask the boys in your class, or the ones at home, for clues about what they want to read. Have a look at mags for boys, or ones that are for teenagers in general, to get some ideas.
2 How is the print media coping with the rapid development of online social media? Use examples from this passage and your own ideas to explain your answer.

Extend yourself *(Links to real life or other literature, researching, writing, creating, speaking tasks)*

1 Research a range of women's magzines and create a table comparing this editorial and the others.
2 Present this editorial aloud. Read it with the personality and expression that the writer has intended. Remember to use volume, pause, tone of voice, speed etc to help you in your presentation.

UNIT 30

TEXT TYPE Narrative (extract)
PURPOSE To tell a story
STRUCTURE
1 Orientation – who or what, where or when
2 Complication
3 Series of events
4 Resolution

FEATURES Use of past tense, descriptive language, characters, direct speech

From *The Hunger Games* by Suzanne Collins

All forms of stealing are forbidden in District 12. Punishable by death. But it crossed my mind that there might be something in the rubbish bins, and those were fair game. Perhaps a bone at the butcher's or rotted vegetables at the grocer's, something no one but my family was desperate enough to eat. Unfortunately, the bins had just been emptied.

When I passed the baker's, the smell of fresh bread was so overwhelming I felt dizzy. The ovens were in the back, and a golden glow spilled out of the open kitchen door. I stood mesmerized by the heat and the luscious scent until the rain interfered, running its icy fingers down my back, forcing me back to life. I lifted the lid to the baker's rubbish bin and found it spotlessly, heartlessly bare.

Suddenly a voice was screaming at me and I looked up to see the baker's wife, telling me to move on and did I want her to call the Peacekeepers and how sick she was of having those brats from the Seam pawing through her rubbish. The words were ugly and I had no defence. As I carefully replaced the lid and backed away, I noticed him, a boy with blond hair peering out from behind his mother's back. I'd seen him at school. He was in my year, but I didn't know his name. He stuck with the town kids, so how would I? His mother went back into the bakery, grumbling, but he must have been watching me as I made my way behind the pen that held their pig and leaned against the far side of an old apple tree. The realisation that I'd have nothing to take home had finally sunk in. My knees buckled and I slid down the tree trunk to its roots. It was too much. I was too sick and weak and tired, oh, so tired.

Let them call the Peacekeepers and take us to the community home, I thought. *Or better yet, let me die right here in the rain.*

There was a clatter in the bakery and I heard the woman screaming again and the sound of a blow, and I vaguely wondered what was going on. Feet sloshed towards me through the mud and I thought, *It's her. She's coming to drive me away with a stick.* But it wasn't her. It was the boy. In his arms, he carried two large loaves of bread that must have fallen into the fire because the crusts were scorched black.

His mother was yelling, "Feed it to the pig, you stupid creature! Why not? No one decent will buy burned bread!"

He began to tear off chunks from the burned parts and toss them into the trough, and the front bakery bell rang and the mother disappeared to help a customer.

The boy never even glanced my way, but I was watching him. Because of the bread, because of the red weal that stood out on his cheekbone. What had she hit him with? My parents never hit us. I couldn't even imagine it. The boy took one look back at the bakery as if checking that the coast was clear, then, his attention back on the pig, he threw a loaf of bread in my direction. The second quickly followed, and he sloshed back to the bakery, closing the kitchen door tightly behind him.

I stared at the loaves in disbelief. They were fine, perfect really, except for the burned areas. Did he mean for me to have them? He must have. Because there they were at my feet. Before anyone could witness what had happened I shoved the loaves up under my shirt, wrapped the hunting jacket tightly about me, and walked swiftly away. The heat of the bread burned into my skin, but I clutched it tighter, clinging to life.

On the surface *(Literal comprehension – right-there questions)*

1 What was forbidden in District 12?
2 What was the girl looking for in the rubbish bins?
3 What was her reaction to the smell of fresh bread? Why?
4 Why did the mother hit the boy?

Discovering techniques *(Language structures and features, spelling, grammar, vocabulary)*

1 Find an example of personification in the passage.
2 Find an example of onomatopoeia in the passage.
3 Find one example of direct speech (where the exact words that were spoken are given) and one example of reported speech (another way of saying what someone said) from the passage.
4 Why has the author chosen to use italics for certain sentences?

Search and think *(Inferential and interpretive comprehension)*

1 How does the writer show the reader that the girl is starving?
2 Do you think that the boy dropped the bread on purpose? Explain your thoughts.
3 Why did the boy never look at her?
4 Why did she stare at the loaves of bread in disbelief?
5 What is the importance of the phrase 'clinging to life'?

Hidden depths *(Creative comprehension – responding personally, higher-order-thinking skills, making links)*

1 After the mother had yelled at the girl, the girl says: 'The words were ugly and I had no defence.' Is the woman wrong to scream at the girl? Do you have any sympathy for the woman? Do you think the girl has no defence? Give reasons for your answer.
2 The boy is referred to as being from the 'town' and the girl the 'Seam'. Using words from the text in your answer, explain what you think each of these places is like.
3 Do you think it was hard for the boy to help the girl? What difficulties might he face in doing so?

Extend yourself *(Links to real life or other literature, researching, writing, creating, speaking tasks)*

1 Write a short story of your own about someone helping another person even though it brings trouble to them.
2 Imagine you are in a similar situation to the girl – starving, alone, scared of other people. Describe a moment when you have to act to feed yourself.
3 Imagine you have watched this scene from your bedroom window. The next day a Peacekeeper comes to your house to tell you that the girl has been arrested for stealing bread. What would you tell him?

ISBN 9780170260121

UNIT 31

TEXT TYPE Script (extract)
PURPOSE To entertain
STRUCTURE
1. Orientation – who or what, where and when
2. Complication
3. Series of events
4. Resolution

FEATURES Direct speech, stage directions

PETER: Ioane and I brought glory to the Indian Sports 1D cricket team. Mr Patel K Senior insisted we picked any ice block we wanted from his dairy. Then he gave Ioane a great big bag of lollies for top-scoring with 88 runs. We walked home, arm in arm, extremely happy – until a familiar Holden Kingswood pulled up beside us. Funny how it only ever happened when I was with Ioane.

COP: Hello boys. Where have you been?

IOANE: Playing cricket, constable.

COP: Is that right? Who for?

IOANE: Indian Sports.

COP: Of course you would. Who's the captain of your team? Mr Patel is it?

IOANE: Yes.

COP: What a surprise. Own a fruit shop does he?

IOANE: No. Dairy.

COP: You think you're pretty smart, don't you? Where did you get those ice blocks?

IOANE: Mr Patel gave them to us.

COP: I see, you just walked into Mr Patel's dairy and he handed them over. Then he said, 'here, have some lollies too.'

IOANE: That's right.

COP: What's your name?

IOANE: Ioane Tafioka.

COP: What does your father do, Ioane?

IOANE: He's a seagull.

COP: Are you looking for a hiding?

IOANE: He works at the wharves.

COP: You boys are out late.

IOANE: Game went to the last over.

COP: Do your parents know you're out?

IOANE: No.

COP: *into radio* Two young shoplifters. One offender – Islander about fourteen.

IOANE: I'm ten, sir.

COP: Says he's ten. One Caucasian accomplice – same age. And don't open those lollies.

IOANE: Sorry sir.

PETER: After checking with Mr Patel, the cops dropped us home. Ioane hadn't done anything wrong, but he still got a whack from his mother 'cos she didn't want him getting involved with the police. And while Ioane was a hit on the sports field he wasn't doing as well as me in the classroom. Mum and Dad reckoned I should help him with school work as much as I could.

DAD: Peter, where in the hell have you been?

PETER: At Ioane's.

DAD: But it's half past nine! Your mother's been going crazy. She's out looking for you.

PETER: We were joining the library.

DAD: You already belong.

IOANE: I was helping Ioane join.

DAD: That takes two seconds.

PETER: Not for Mrs Tafioka. She can't read. I had to wait for Mr Tafioka to come home.

DAD: And?

PETER: He was drunk.

DAD: Oh Jesus. You could have let us know.

PETER: I was only trying to help, but it's pretty hard joining someone up with the library when their father starts singing all the time and their mother can't write and we're trying to get a book and it's not my fault.

Peter bursts into tears.

DAD: I'm sorry. Did you join him up in the end?

PETER: Yeah. I filled the forms in myself and forged Mr and Mrs Tafioka's signature.

DAD: Well done. You're a good friend to Ioane, but don't tell your mother about the signatures. Was Mr Tafioka okay?

PETER: Yeah, but I have to see him first thing tomorrow morning.

DAD: What for?

PETER: He's going to pay me fifty cents to do his income tax.

ISBN 9780170260121

On the surface *(Literal comprehension – right-there questions)*

1 What did Mr Patel give the boys and why?
2 What does Ioane's father do for a living?
3 How old does the cop think Ioane is? How old is he?
4 How does Peter solve the problem of enrolling Ioane in the library?

Discovering techniques *(Language structures and features, spelling, grammar, vocabulary)*

1 Peter has two roles in the play. What are they?
2 Look up the word 'seagull' in a dictionary. What does it mean in this context?
3 The cop sometimes says the opposite of what he means. Give one example of this and identify the language technique.

Search and think *(Inferential and interpretive comprehension)*

1 Why is the policeman named COP?
2 Are there other stereotypes in the scene?
3 How does the scene try to deflate these stereotypes?

Hidden depths *(Creative comprehension – responding personally, higher-order-thinking skills, making links)*

1 What does the way Ioane speaks to the policeman tell you about him and his upbringing?
2 What is the scene saying about education?
3 This scene is set in the past. Does it relate in any way to New Zealand today?

Extend yourself *(Links to real life or other literature, researching, writing, creating, speaking tasks)*

1 Write a scene of this play for yourself using the characters of Peter and Ioane and think of another situation they could have experienced together.
2 What techniques could the writers use to illustrate the different ways of speech of these new migrant Pacific Island characters?
3 Read the whole play.
4 Perform scenes from the play.

ISBN 9780170260121

UNIT
32

TEXT TYPE Poem
PURPOSE To express ideas in precise and powerful language
STRUCTURE Lines, rhyme, rhythm, verses
FEATURES Careful word choice for meaning and sound, figurative language, verse, rhyme, imagery

Tawera

We strode like gods down the slope
over the stile
across the stones
to the swimming hole

the summer sun drove everyone
to that sanctuary
lying beneath the branches of the willow
those initiated into manhood shed their
leather jackets
with fist on the back and dove from the
rock face.

Forever they would fall
twisting, yelling
knees pulled into chests
an explosion of water rising into the air
they disappeared
re-emerging to the kids' cheers.

Where are they now?

Robert got his stomach pumped after
swallowing petrol;
he was never the same.
Andrew got shot by a rival gang;
the same age as me.

It's deceptive those country roads
that merge with sunlight to create a mirage
where if you go too far you fall off the world
or so it seems.

I used to dream of those country roads
tongue and eyes ecstatic
barefoot in the mud
while the city team had boots...

Have I changed
become a townie?
I have lost the Reo
can only say ' Kia Ora, Kei te pehea?'
one day soon I will return
to see the smallness of things
where once everything was large.

It's true what you said, Kuia,
the river at every turn, there is a taniwha.

Simon Williamson

ISBN 9780170260121

On the surface *(Literal comprehension – right-there questions)*

1 What time of year is the poem set?
2 Where were the teenagers going?
3 What was the image on the back of some of the jackets?
4 Why did Robert need to have his stomach pumped?
5 What line tells you there was a crowd watching them jump off the rock face?

Discovering techniques *(Language structures and features, spelling, grammar, vocabulary)*

1 What technique dominates the first stanza?
2 'We strode like gods down the slope' is example of what figure of speech?
Can you write a definition of the following words using your own prior knowledge?
Once you have done so, use the Internet to check yourself. Alter where required.
a Kia ora b Kuia c Taniwha
3 Use a dictionary to find the meanings of the following words as they are used in the text:
a sanctuary b initiated c mirage.

Search and think *(Inferential and interpretive comprehension)*

1 What does the phrase 'We strode like gods down the slope' suggest about the group of teenagers?
2 What do the *lines 'those initiated into manhood shed their leather jackets/with fist on the back'* refer to?
3 Which line divides the time of the poem between past and present?
4 What do you think the poet is referring to in the following stanza?

I used to dream of those country roads
tongue and eyes ecstatic
barefoot in the mud
while the city team had boots...

5 What do you think the poet means when he says 'one day soon I will return/to see the smallness of things/where once everything was large'?
6 Explain in two sentences what you think the poem is about.

Hidden depths *(Creative comprehension – responding personally, higher-order-thinking skills, making links)*

1 What does the poem say about the choices young men have to make?
2 What does the poet remember about his youth in this poem? Try to give examples to support your answer.

Extend yourself *(Links to real life or other literature, researching, writing, creating, speaking tasks)*

1 Write a poem or a descriptive passage about a particular moment you remember from a summer in your childhood.
2 Explore the idea of the taniwha. Find examples of how a taniwha has influenced a person's life, if you can.
3 Using the place you live in as your focus, what is it like to play rugby (or another sport) as a teenager in your community? If you do not play sport yourself you will need to interview some teenagers who do!

ISBN 9780170260121

UNIT 33

TEXT TYPE Discussion

PURPOSE To inform and persuade by presenting evidence and opinions about more than one side of an issue

STRUCTURE
1. Opening statement presenting the issue
2. Arguments or evidence for different points of view
3. Concluding recommendation

FEATURES Facts and figures, logical reasoning, examples, persuasive or emotive language

Kevin Milne's thoughts on … self-service checkouts

Call me a bit sad, but since I left television, I've come to love time spent in my supermarket. The checkout 'girls' are my best friends, whom I send cards to on holiday.

I go to a flash supermarket in order to also get the 'packing girls' or, sometimes, blokes. It's more people to chat to and they stick everything in bags for me while I talk. These wonderful people are what I pay top supermarket dollar to access. So what the hell is my supermarket trying to do now? Divert me to their new self-serve checkouts. In effect, what the owner's saying to me is, 'Kevin, we'd like to lay off some of your friends on the checkout. It would save us some serious dosh. We can teach you to check out your own stuff. We'll even give you lessons for the first week or two.'

I want to say to the supermarket owner, 'And what's in this for me? If I use self-serve, do you take 10 percent off my bill? Tell you what. I'll do my own packing if you change the name of your store to Pak'New World, and charge the same prices as that dingy den down the road.'

But I don't, because I hate conflict. Instead, I flat out refuse to use the self-serve checkouts. Nor will I eat any food my wife checks out through them. She says I'm being stubborn. She's right.

Remember when you used to call up a business and someone would answer the phone. That was when there were telephonists. They prided themselves on answering all calls within the first three rings. They were the unheralded backbone of every large organisation. So we got rid of them.

Some idiot came up with the call centre. These were huge operations based off shore and taking calls for several businesses at the same time. They knew nothing about any of them of course. Another Einstein realised you still had to pay people in India and the Philippines. So they started laying off call centre telephonists, too, and along came one of the telecommunications' most irritating breakthroughs – the recorded message. It took a few decades to refine itself, but the recorded message now allows nobody to answer their phone.

As I said at the start, self-service – doing the work yourself and paying someone for the privilege – has only just begun. You must fight it. Take part and you're simply digging a hole for yourself.

I mean that literally. Funeral directors are working on self-service burials as we speak.

  ISBN 9780170260121

On the surface *(Literal comprehension – right-there questions)*

1 What job did Kevin used to have?
2 What recent change at his local supermarket does he dislike?
3 What job does he say used to be the backbone of a business?
4 Which countries are given as examples of where call centres are located?
5 What does Kevin pay 'top supermarket dollar' to access?

Discovering techniques *(Language structures and features, spelling, grammar, vocabulary)*

1 Find one example of each of the following techniques:
   a Alliteration
   b Rhetorical question
   c Colloquial language
   d Cliché.
2 Use a dictionary to find the meanings of the following words as they are used in the text:
   a divert
   b unheralded.
3 Why is the word 'girls' in inverted commas?

Search and think *(Inferential and interpretive comprehension)*

1 Why does Kevin enjoy going to the supermarket?
2 Is his wife correct? Is he stubborn? Explain your answer.
3 How does the writer achieve a conversational tone?
4 The humour of the passage comes sometimes from exaggeration. Find two examples of exaggeration.
5 'Another Einstein…' Who was Einstein? Why does Kevin use this phrase?
6 What does the writer dislike most about these changes in service?

Hidden depths *(Creative comprehension – responding personally, higher-order-thinking skills, making links)*

1 You use a supermarket. What is your opinion about self-service checkouts?
2 What other ways do businesses try to save money by do-it-yourself methods?

Extend yourself *(Links to real life or other literature, researching, writing, creating, speaking tasks)*

1 Conduct a survey among people you know who go shopping. Who likes self-service and why?
2 Write an article for a teens magazine about the highs and lows of working in a supermarket.
3 Write a short story from the perspective of a supermarket packer about one day's work experiences.

ISBN 9780170260121

UNIT 34

TEXT TYPE Narrative (extract)
PURPOSE To tell a story
STRUCTURE
1 Orientation – who or what, where or when
2 Complication
3 Series of events
4 Resolution

FEATURES Use of past tense, descriptive language, characters, direct speech, narrative voice

From *Heriot* by Margaret Mahy

Among the ruins, late cabbages, carrots and turnips grew in straight lines, overlooked by five lions with scrolled manes and smiling faces. Earlier in the year these lions had worn wigs of green leaves and scarlet flowers, but now the bean stems were brittle, and the flowers were gone. All that remained were larger, dry pods rattling with the seeds of next year's crop, and a few tattered leaves.

It was autumn but the gardener was still working up and down between his remaining rows of plants, his bare back shining like copper in the autumn sunlight, his long black hair tied back with a plaited ribbon of flax. As he worked he whispered under his breath, smiling into the crumbling soil. His name was Heriot Tarbas and he was twelve years old.

As he worked he sang a little, then whispered again, happy at home on his farm, in his own place, among his own people. During the last three years the catastrophic headaches, the twisting fits, which had marked his entire childhood, had become much rarer. Of course the dreams hung on. He still dreamed that dream – the one in which he found himself sitting on the wide windowsill of an alien building looking in at a boy several years older than he was and sending in an urgent message ... 'Know me! Know me. I'll protect you until then, but you have to recognise me when the time comes. Then it'll be your job to save me. I'll need you and you'll need me.' That dream, along with other less defined ones, certainly hung on, but at least he was growing out of the old feeling that something ravenous was feeding on him and tearing him into two. Perhaps in time, the dreams would fade and disappear and he would become an ordinary male like his brother and cousins, just as hairy and just as strong.

A farm cat stalked towards him, sniffing at the freshly turned earth, and Heriot scooped it up, scratching it under the chin and staring deeply into its yellowish eyes; and as he did so, someone said his private conversations with cats and gardens shouldn't be overheard.

His sister Baba was looking over the wall behind him. Heriot looked back cautiously. Since she had grown up, and been pulled in from the fields to work in the kitchen and dairy, she always seemed to be blaming him for something. But on this occasion at least, she was excited and cheerful.

Heriot had one particular eye – his left eye – that he called his puzzled eye. It didn't always see straight. Now he covered it with his left hand and stared back at his sister, knowing she had come into the garden to tell him something exciting.

'The Travellers have arrived,' she announced. 'Old Jen sent me to bring you in. But don't think you're getting out of work. You'll be given some other job, that's all.'

She grinned and vanished. Heriot cleaned his spade and hoe, then set off down the path that led from the garden to the walled courtyard of his sprawling home. He and his mother, the family herb woman, had planted ferns around the outside of the courtyard wall to keep witches at bay, interspersing them with daisies, well-known sun signs, now working their way into a prodigal autumn flowering.

The house had been built within the walls of a ruined castle, but these days it seemed to have become part of the castle, growing naturally out of the stone shell, for any of the first rooms that were still intact were either lived in, or used for storage. Beyond those original, uneven walls, built of huge blocks of stone, Heriot could glimpse a dairy and an old barn, alongside the roof of a new one. Then, beyond all those roofs and walls, broad fields sloped upwards, patching the hillside until, towards the top, the hill shrugged itself casually out of the farm's control. From the very top of the hill the black rock Draevo, though eyeless, looked back at Heriot as darkly as it had ever since he could remember.

ISBN 9780170260121

On the surface *(Literal comprehension – right-there questions)*

1 At what time of year is this scene set?
2 Who is the gardener?
3 What can you tell about Heriot Tarbas's appearance?
4 Who is Baba and where does she work?
5 Where has Heriot's home been built?

Discovering techniques *(Language structures and features, spelling, grammar, vocabulary)*

1 The writer uses two words as adjectives to describe the lions' manes and faces. What are these words and what do they tell you about the lions?
2 A simile is used to describe Heriot when he is first introduced. What is that simile and what does it tell you?
3 The black rock, Draevo, is described as looking back at Heriot 'darkly'. What technique is this? What effect is the writer intending by using it?

Search and think *(Inferential and interpretive comprehension)*

1 Is Heriot happy? How can you tell?
2 What does Heriot hope for his future?
3 What can you tell about Baba's attitude towards her brother?

Hidden depths *(Creative comprehension – responding personally, higher-order-thinking skills, making links)*

1 What have you learnt about what makes Heriot different from his family?
2 What do the final two paragraphs of the passage tell you about Heriot's world?

Extend yourself *(Links to real life or other literature, researching, writing, creating, speaking tasks)*

1 Write a scene where Heriot meets the boy he has dreamed about.
2 Create a map of Heriot's world.
3 Create a picture to illustrate Heriot's double life.
4 Write a drama scene where Baba overhears Heriot speaking to an animal.
5 Read the novel.

UNIT
35

TEXT TYPE Poem
PURPOSE To express ideas in precise and powerful language
STRUCTURE Lines, rhyme, rhythm, verses
FEATURES Careful word choice for meaning and sound, figurative language, verse, rhyme, imagery

Acquainted with the Night

I have been one acquainted with the night.
I have walked out in rain – and back in rain.
I have outwalked the furthest city light.

I have looked down the saddest city lane.
I have passed by the watchman on his beat
And dropped my eyes, unwilling to explain.

I have stood still and stopped the sound of feet
When far away an interrupted cry
Came over houses from another street,

But not to call me back or say good-bye;
And further still at an unearthly height,
O luminary clock against the sky

Proclaimed the time was neither wrong nor right.
I have been one acquainted with the night.

by Robert Frost

ISBN 9780170260121

On the surface *(Literal comprehension – right-there questions)*

1 When and where does the man go walking?
2 When he stops walking, what is he listening for?
3 What is the clock? Why is it described as 'luminary'?

Discovering techniques *(Language structures and features, spelling, grammar, vocabulary)*

1 What does the word 'acquainted' mean? What does the use of the word suggest to you?
2 The poem uses two superlative adjectives. Identify them.
3 Work out the rhyme and rhythm pattern of the poem.
4 What is this 14-line structure called? (Research the answer if you do not know).

Search and think *(Inferential and interpretive comprehension)*

1 What is a watchman's job, do you think? What happens when the man out walking meets the watchman?
2 What do lines 7-10 suggest about the man's life?

Hidden depths *(Creative comprehension – responding personally, higher-order-thinking skills, making links)*

1 What might the 'night' suggest in terms of a person's psychology?
2 How does he know that one lane in the city is the saddest?
3 Explain what you think the lines about the luminary clock suggest about the man's life/our world.

Extend yourself *(Links to real life or other literature, researching, writing, creating, speaking tasks)*

1 Personal response to a poem is important. What is your personal response to this poem?
2 Find another poem by Robert Frost. Explain what it means to you.
3 Look for another rhyming poem. Identify its rhyme and rhythm pattern.
4 Create a short poem of your own. Try to create a regular rhyme and/or rhythm.

UNIT 36

TEXT TYPE Newspaper article
PURPOSE To persuade by putting forward an argument or particular point of view
STRUCTURE
1 Point of view stated
2 Justifications of argument in a logical order
3 Summing up of argument

FEATURES Facts and figures, logical reasoning, examples, persuasive or emotive language

It may be English but it's not always as we know it

by Stewart Riddle

English is rapidly becoming a lingua franca in international communication for commerce and trade, education, science, international relations and tourism.

It is the fastest growing language in the world, with more people speaking English than ever before. School children in India and China are learning English at a staggering rate as their countries emphasise the importance of English as a ticket to participating in the global economy.

So why then do we continue to link this evolving internationalising language with a small island in Europe that once upon a time controlled the world?

Perhaps it is about time we got rid of the 'English' and start calling it something else – international, standard or common language?

It is important to understand that there is not one English language; there are many. In fact, in Australia we don't even speak and write English. We use Standard Australian English, which is not the same English that you might find in the United Kingdom, the United States, India or China.

There are countless blends, pidgins, creoles and mixed English languages. At the same time that English is becoming the language of internationalisation, it is also becoming localised in different parts of the world as multiple world Englishes flourish.

A sociocultural perspective on language considers the impacts of regional dialects, national standards and conventions, slang, different pronunciations and the use of communication technologies such as mobile telephones, texting and email. Our use of English depends on the contexts, audiences and purposes we are using it for.

Spoken English differs from written English. There are different ways of using written English depending on the formality and genre of writing.

English is an 'open source' language, with hybrid forms appearing all over the globe as different peoples blend English with other languages.

Some interesting points about English languages: there are more non-native speakers of English than native speakers; nearly four out of five English-speaking interactions happen between non-native speakers of English; most research is shared in English-language journals; English is the number one language used on Internet sites; English is the language of international aviation; and most literature is published in English or translated from English into other languages.

The rise of English comes with several concerns, including questions of cultural hegemony and postcolonial criticisms. While it is easy to shrug off such criticisms with the argument that English is necessary for social mobility, economic prosperity and education, there remain many unanswered questions around the social and cultural impacts of English as a global language.

For example, the use of English in the internationalisation of research and higher education comes at a cost to local knowledge and languages, as academics in places such as Japan, China and Germany compete with scholars from the UK and the US to publish in English-language research journals.

Even in France, which is renowned for its linguistic protectiveness, English is gaining ground in its universities, with 83 per cent of French lecturers using English in their field of research.

There is a real tragedy in the loss of language diversity as English takes over, placing other languages at risk of extinction. This has been acknowledged and efforts are being made to preserve indigenous languages in places such as Papua New Guinea, Brazil and Australia. However, is this enough? Are we destroying more than language through the rise of English as the international standard?

That said, there is some sadness in the idea that we might be the last generation of travellers who experience those amusing and sometimes awkward moments when attempting to order food or ask for directions in a country where everyone doesn't speak English.

ISBN 9780170260121

On the surface *(Literal comprehension – right-there questions)*

1. What areas of communication between countries is English used for?
2. What reasons for learning English as a second language does the writer give?
3. Create a five-bullet point list of facts about the use of English in your own words.
4. In which countries does the writer say indigenous languages are being preserved?

Discovering techniques *(Language structures and features, spelling, grammar, vocabulary)*

1. Look up the phrase 'lingua franca'. What does it mean?
2. Why is English described as an 'open source' language?
3. The headline of this article alludes to a television programme. Which one? Explain.

Search and think *(Inferential and interpretive comprehension)*

1. What communication methods affect our use of English?
2. What concerns the writer about the rise of English as the international standard?

Hidden depths *(Creative comprehension – responding personally, higher-order-thinking skills, making links)*

1. What is the indigenous language of New Zealand? Is it being preserved?
2. The writer says Australians use Standard Australian English. Do we here in New Zealand use New Zealand English? Support your response.
3. Has the use of the mobile phone, texting and email affected your use of English?

Extend yourself *(Links to real life or other literature, researching, writing, creating, speaking tasks)*

1. Interview an international student (or two from different countries) at your school. Ask them why they want to learn English.
2. Research New Zealand English by reading literature written by New Zealand authors and/or watching New Zealand-made television programmes or websites. What language features make it clear that it is New Zealand made?
3. What do you think? Should we rename the language we speak?

Language terms

Abstract nouns: abstract nouns refer to qualities or things that we cannot see, hear or touch. For instance: aroha, hate, hunger or humour.

Adjectival phrase: an adjective describes the noun so an adjectival phrase is a group of words whose job is to describe the noun.

Adjectives: adjectives are describing words.

Adverb: an adverb tells us how, when or where an action takes place.

Adverbial phrase: an adverb describes the how, where or when of the verb so an adverbial phrase is a group of words whose job it is to describe the verb.

Alliteration: alliteration is the repetition of consonant sounds, in a sequence of words.

Antonym: an antonym is a word that is opposite in meaning to a given word.

Apostrophe: the apostrophe has two main purposes. The first is to show ownership. The second to show where one or more letters is missed out in a contraction (making two words into one).

Assonance: assonance is the deliberate repetition of the same vowel sound followed by a different consonant sound.

Brackets: brackets are most commonly used to include extra information within a sentence.

Capital letter: every new sentence must start with a capital letter.

Cliché: a cliché is a trite, dull expression that has lost its originality and humour through constant use.

Collective noun: noun that refers to a group or collection of similar people, animals or things.

Colloquialism: colloquial language is relaxed and informal language that is used in common conversation.

Colon: the colon (:) introduces more information or shows divisions.

Comma: the comma tells the reader when to take a short pause in a sentence.

Conjunction: a conjunction is a word that joins words or sentences.

Dash: the dash has three main purposes. The first is to indicate a sudden change of thought. The second is to lead to the unexpected. The third is to give extra information.

Direct speech: this means the exact words that someone has spoken and are shown by speech marks " " or ' '.

Exclamation mark: an exclamation mark is used at the end of a sentence. It shows strong feeling.

Full stop: a full stop brings an end to a sentence.

Hyphens: hyphens are used to join two or more words to make a compound word and to divide a word at the end of a line.

Jargon: jargon is specialised language used by people who work together or share a common interest.

Metaphor: a metaphor is a comparison, where one thing is said to *be* another.

Minor sentence: a minor sentence is a group of words that do not make complete sense on their own. Usually it needs a verb to make it complete.

Noun: a noun is a naming word.

Onomatopoeia: onomatopoeia is when the sound of the word imitates or suggests the meaning or noise of the action described.

Paragraph: the purpose of the paragraph is to group sentences that have something in common, to show a change of speaker during dialogue or to show other important changes.

Personal pronoun: a personal pronoun is a word that stands in place of the name of a person or persons.

Personification: personification is when a non-human thing is given human characteristics.

Phrase: a phrase is a group of words without a completed verb. It does not make complete sense on its own.

Possessive pronouns: possessive pronouns are words that signify ownership.

Prefix: a prefix is a group of letters added to the beginning of a word to change its meaning or form a new word.

Preposition: a preposition is a word that tells us the position or place of something in relation to something else. For example: The cat sat *on* the mat.

Pronouns: pronouns are used instead of nouns when referring to people or things.

Proper nouns: proper nouns are nouns that refer to a specific person, place, object or period of time.

Pun: a pun is an expression that plays on different meanings of the same word or phrase.

Question mark: a question mark is used at the end of a sentence that asks a direct question.

Reported speech: this is when what has been said is told to the reader (is reported). There are no speech marks around reported speech.

Rhyme: rhyme is the repetition of words with similar sounds.

Semi-colon: a semi-colon (;) is used to break up long sentences and lists, or to join clauses that are closely related.

Simile: a simile is a phrase that compares two things, using 'like' or 'as' or 'than'.

Simple sentence: a simple sentence is a group of words, including a verb, that makes sense on its own.

Speech marks: speech marks are used to show the words being said by a speaker.

Suffix: a suffix is one or more letters added to the end of a word to alter its meaning.

Synonym: a synonym is a word identical or very similar in meaning to another word.

Verb: a verb is a doing word.

ISBN 9780170260121